Stratas

Stratas

An Affectionate Tribute

Harry Rasky

based on his film
StrataSphere

Toronto New York
OXFORD UNIVERSITY PRESS
1988

To Pearl Krasnyansky Rasky,
my mother, and all the immigrant mothers
who gave us life.

Oxford University Press, 70 Wynford Drive, Don Mills, Ontario, M3C 1J9

Toronto Oxford New York Delhi Bombay Calcutta Madras
Karachi Petaling Jaya Singapore Hong Kong Tokyo Nairobi
Dar es Salaam Cape Town Melbourne Auckland

and associated companies in
Berlin Ibadan

CANADIAN CATALOGUING IN PUBLICATION DATA

Rasky, Harry, 1928–
Stratas
ISBN 0-19-540598-6
1. Stratas, Teresa. 2. Singers—Canada—Biography.
3. Actresses—Canada—Biography. 4. StrataSphere
(Motion picture). I. Stratas, Teresa. II. Title.

ML420.S77R38 1988   782.1′092′4   C88-094603-4

FRONTISPIECE *As Violetta in Franco Zeffirelli's film of* La Traviata, *1983.*

Contents

Just as the year 1985 was coming to a close, a brief item appeared in the entertainment section of the Sunday *New York Times*, under the heading "50 Outstanding C.D. Releases," by music critic John Rockwell: "WEILL: Songs. Teresa Stratas, soprano. A rehearing of these powerful, poignant performances makes her withdrawal from the public eye seem all the sadder." The haunting face of Teresa Stratas, caught in mid-note, glowed from the page, with a caption repeating the theme: "Weill songs, poignantly sung." And that was all.

Behind those words was a story worthy of a book. The words reminded me, if reminding was necessary, of how like an opera Teresa's life has been—an unpredictable plot filled with suspense, fateful encounters, and passionate arias.

We who have not been "blessed or cursed" with the gift of music, to borrow a phrase from Teresa, cannot know the pressures felt by those who have. But we can hear, appreciate and applaud—even if, in the end, we can never fully understand. Seven years have passed since I first met Teresa, who is the subject of one of my most important films, *StrataSphere*. There is no way for me to tell about the Teresa I know without sketching in the background of our filming, so I won't try to remove myself from these pages. And it is encounters, not explanations, that this book will offer.

Music has played a dominant role in all my films, just as it has in my life. My father was a shoychet and cantor, one of those special musicians who carry their instrument within them. I recall walking home from the synagogue—"the McKay Street Schul" as we called it, in Toronto—after the service for Yom Kippur, the most holy of holy days. My father had sung the epic chant of mourning, Kol Nidre, and I had watched him struggle with what I thought was God's own hymn. He was a small lion of a man, with blazing red hair and beard. We walked silently for a time, then he paused and asked: "Nu? What?" I expected him to ask for sacred thoughts. Instead he asked:

In the Metropolitan Opera's Mahagonny, 1979. Critic John Ardoin wrote, "Stratas' performance of Jenny ranks among the handful of performances streaked with genius on the current operatic stage."

"Nu? How was I?" The prayer and the performer were mixed. The song and the singer were the same. Though I've never had the gift of song, I always admired it in my father. In many ways it is my most vivid memory of home: either silence or song, and seldom anything in between. Perhaps that experience was part of the appeal of making a film about Teresa, and then this book.

One day in early 1981, my wife Arlene, who has always had a sixth sense for finding subjects that satisfy, called my attention to a beautifully composed piece in *The New Yorker* by Winthrop Sargeant. In fact she was so taken with the article that she was reading it aloud to our children, Adam and Holly, as if it were a nursery tale or a yarn by the Brothers Grimm. It had that kind of adventure about it. Appearing under the heading "Profiles," it had as its title one word—"Presence"—and a simple line drawing of a woman with, as the author observed, "beseeching" eyes that seemed "to express a need of help and sympathy." As Mr. Sargeant told of Teresa's beginnings, all that was missing was the "once upon a time": "About fifty years ago a nearly illiterate young shepherd from the mountains of Crete named Emmanuel Stratas (his Cretan name was Stratakis) emigrated to Canada, where he settled in Toronto. There he met a young Cretan woman named Argero Terezakis, who had been imported to North America to marry a rich Cretan-American. That prospect did not appeal to her, and before long Emmanuel and Argero married. From their union were born Nicholas Stratas, who became a psychiatrist, was deputy commissioner of the North Carolina Department of Mental Health for a time, and is now in very successful private practice; Mary Garofalakis, who became principal of the Greek-American Institute, an elementary school in the Bronx primarily for children of Greek descent, affiliated with the Greek Orthodox Church; and Anastasia Stratas, who, under the name Teresa Stratas, is one of the most celebrated divas in the current world of opera."

The article went on to spell out what it was that made Teresa special. "Aside from her vocal and thespian abilities, Stratas has the mysterious faculty known as 'presence'—the faculty that arrests one's attention the instant its possessor appears onstage. It is a quality that she has shared with the late Maria Callas, another North American of Greek origin, and with George London, the great Canadian-born baritone. Even when she is standing still, the eyes of the audience are riveted on her." I was fascinated. Here was clearly an unusual person, someone with not only a mysterious presence and an extraordinary story, but a ready-made bond in common with me: we came from the same home town. I had the beginning of an idea for a film.

I felt some timidity about approaching Teresa because I knew so little about opera. For me it was synonymous with Saturday-afternoon Texaco broadcasts on the radio, during the Depression years in Toronto. After pushing our bicycles through the slush and mud of Toronto's streets all week, on Saturdays we were allowed one infringement of the Sabbath disciplinary laws. Lights could not be turned on or off, the stove could not be touched, neither driving nor movement on mechanical transport was permitted—yet my father turned a deaf ear to allow us kids, crowded into the apartment above the store on St. Clair Avenue, to listen to the opera. Wagner was splendid to sleep by, *La Traviata* a comfort to aching muscles. Occasionally you were awakened by the opera quiz, but that didn't matter. The Met was a soothing constant for us and no doubt thousands of other kids, as well as their parents, across North America.

Those were the memories that stirred in me as I wrote my first letter to Teresa, whom I imagined as some *grande dame* enveloped by the glamor of the Metropolitan, a world of crystal chandeliers, ice-cold champagne, and Russian caviar. I told Teresa in my first note that it would be a chance to tell the story of immigrant experience, and that if she approved, she would join the list of notable people about whom I had made films—Marc Chagall, Tennessee Williams and Mikhail Baryshnikov.

A brief note came, agreeing to meet with me.

The apartment building she lives in, not far from the Met on the upper west side of New York, is an ornate, beaux-arts affair that seems to be all memory. On entering the lobby, an echoing marbled area of poodles on leashes and shopping carts full of laundry and men carrying violins and brass horns, you have a sense of fifty years ago. A small orchestra could be rehearsing in it and you feel that no one would take much notice. Music seems to have seeped long ago into its wide-planked floors.

Framed by high, plum-colored double doors, the woman who greeted me was tiny but large in her life force. Teresa's vitality was unmistakable. She seemed to circle me, even as we stood still and greeted each other. Sargeant's description seemed absolutely correct: "Her face resembled a Minoan mask of perhaps 2000 B.C. The huge eyes are dark—so dark as to resemble the eyeholes of a mask. The nose descends from the forehead without a notch between the eyes, as do the noses of figures in frescoes and statues at Knossos and Mycenae. The mouth is at the same time sensual and determined. . . . Although she appears to be in her twenties, Stratas looks like a waif." Yet I also detected a commanding look in the beseeching eyes.

This tiny giant weighs in at about ninety-five pounds and stands five feet tall. Yet her constant motion gives you the sense that she is also looking down at you. There is an openness in her privacy, a welcome in her distance, an instant invitation that seems to say, Come, be with me—but on my terms. An absolute certainty, yet ready to respect and be challenged by a conflicting intellect. A challenge is there even in "How are you?"—the low voice insists on an honest answer.

The vivid colored robes that Teresa wears around her spacious apartment are so loose-fitting they seem more like dwellings than dresses. Her rapid and expression-charged arm movements give you the sense she might just sail off. The eyes focus on you so deeply that you are immediately, totally involved.

Teresa expressed great reluctance about the film project. She values her privacy. (True—she lives with the secretiveness of a safety box in a vault, constantly changing her unlisted telephone numbers; even the Met could have difficulty calling her on the phone.) But I was mindful of an old Yiddish proverb: *Ibergekumene tsores iz gut tsu dertseylin* (troubles overcome are good to tell). Before leaving, I gave her a copy of my memoirs, *Nobody Swings on Sunday*. Basically a chronicle of my work, it also contains an opening chapter about the pain and poverty of my own Toronto beginnings. This humorous recollection of early days in Toronto brought us together. She told me by phone that she had enjoyed discussing the opening chapter with her sister, Mary.

My second letter to her, in early May, began:

> Dear Teresa:
> I am most pleased that we are finally having our second session as confirmed with you by phone yesterday.
> It is my hope that I may buy you lunch; might I suggest the Russian Tea Room if that is convenient or anywhere else you like.
> Perhaps we will run the *Tennessee Williams' South* film to give you an idea of approach.
> I hope this letter finds you well. We are all considering the film with you a major and important project and are excited ...

The Russian Tea Room had long been one of my haunts, ever since 1956, when I had lived opposite it for one season, in a sublet at the famous Osborne Apartments. In those days the restaurant had a dingy splendor. Paint and advertising have changed the atmosphere and prices, but it is still a hang-out for musical—and showbiz—personalities. I soon learned that Teresa avoided all the trappings of glamor. Silken splendor was for onstage. Off, she moved about New York by foot, or on cross-town buses, passing for a sales clerk or, in her Chinese worker's cap, even a newsboy. Lunch was a sliced pear in her apartment.

The screening of *Tennessee Williams' South* was unquestionably the turning point in Teresa's decision to go through with the project. The Williams film was my own favorite, because of its emotional power. Teresa immediately felt the soul of the man, his obvious passion reaching her deeply. Still, she questioned whether she, as an interpreter of other people's music, could offer the same force. But I argued that we were all trying to explain the universe in our own way.

Months would pass before the moment of truth came, when I would sit down with Teresa—camera running—to talk about her life. As usual, I had prepared for it by reading every available book or magazine article about my subject, by speaking to people who know—or knew—her, and by viewing every available example of her work.

Even when the date was finally set—the week of November 18, 1981—and I felt confident that not much could go wrong, an odd sense of early frost seemed to surround our enterprise, which none of us who worked on the film will forget.

In addition to all the normal production problems, Lotte Lenya, star of *The Threepenny Opera* and champion of the music of her late husband, composer Kurt Weill, lay dying at the age of eighty-three. Her constant companion in those last days and nights was Teresa. When we arrived in New York, she broke the news that she wanted to spend as many hours as possible with Lenya. The two had met when Teresa took on the role of Jenny in the Metropolitan Opera's 1979 production of the Kurt Weill-Bertolt Brecht classic *The Rise and Fall of the City of Mahagonny*. Then, on January 5, 1980, in a concert given at New York's Whitney Museum of American Art to commemorate the eightieth anniversary of Weill's birth, she had first performed some of the unpublished songs that became a record—the same dazzling record that caused *The New York Times* to evoke its memory three years after its original release. Lenya, of course, had been taken with Teresa, and referred to her as "my dream Jenny."

That November, while Lenya was dying, and Teresa was rehearsing Franco Zeffirelli's new production of *La Bohème*, I arrived with a camera crew.

I picked Teresa up in the evening, after her vigil, in the lobby of Lenya's east-side apartment. She was dressed in what I called her

newsboy outfit, a kind of parka and a Chinese cap, a tiny statement in blue, with only her red-orange hair curling from the cap to reveal a most attractive woman. I walked with her in silence for some blocks, trying not to interfere with the haze of emotions surrounding her. I noticed the quick step of those around us, men and women smartly turned out for stylish dinners. There is always a mood of special expectation as New York prepares for Thanksgiving, and they seemed filled with it.

"Lenya told me so many things," Teresa said quietly at last.

I did not ask what things. Instead I asked if she was afraid to walk the New York streets at night.

"Never," she replied. (Indeed she had been mugged in a famous episode, not far from her apartment. Little did those would-be thugs know the force they were tackling. Teresa proceeded on stage with a slightly blackened eye.)

We boarded a cross-town bus and passed through Central Park, Despite Teresa's newsboy outfit, a young woman recognized her and asked if she would be singing at the Met this season. Teresa politely explained her schedule.

We walked down Broadway to her apartment building, passing fresh-fruit stands and delicatessens alive with seedy night-time magic. In the lobby the desk man looked up to note her arrival quite casually. After all, at one time or another, this building has been the home of Caruso, Toscanini, and Sarah Bernhardt.

Seated on the couch of her apartment, we shared a meal of bananas and nuts, nothing like the grand dinner I'd hoped to buy for her to mark the onset of filming; I learned early that Teresa seems never to eat at all. I suggested that perhaps the next day we might do the central filmed interview.

"Not yet," she said, "No. Not yet."

I absentmindedly ate some nuts without removing the shells. The economics of carrying a film crew across the border, and waiting to begin, was staggering.

"Not yet? When?" I asked, trying not to show my concern.

"Later. Maybe later in the week."

She smiled and I studied her smile. I just smiled back, and agreed that next day we would meet backstage at the Met.

Meanwhile, in an effort to keep the camera crew occupied, I had instructed them to film the exterior of the building. The stage entrance of the new Met at Lincoln Center could be part of a factory anywhere—the cement ramps that lead to it make it seem more like a place to ship crates from than to observe singers. But I could feel

With Lotte Lenya, after the Whitney Museum concert, 1980. "The quintessential Weillian female," wrote critic Pamela Bloom of Teresa, "a whorl of destructive vulnerability, momentarily sanctified by the classical technique that encased it."

the pride Teresa had in showing me her locker and dressing room. Rehearsals were going on for several operas simultaneously—a factory for fantasy.

I met Franco Zeffirelli for the first time. He was involved in staging a scene and he viewed me suspiciously, but I could tell his prime concern was pleasing Teresa. Franco's is a life of opera. He is all grand theatrical gesture, a lover of the lavish in design and theater. At the end of the tour, I suggested setting the date for our filmed conversation, but Teresa was still preoccupied with Lotte Lenya.

The following day Teresa consented to let us follow her walk from her apartment to the Met. It was more of a run than walk. I never knew my camera crew to move so fast. I tried to slow her down and asked what the city meant to her.

"I don't know. I hate cities. However, if you're going to be in any city, this is the city to be in—it is the city of the world. It's the most horrible and it's the greatest city in the world. I just came back from India—you see a lot of starving people there. Here, if you walk by and see ten people, you feel seven or eight of them are starving spiritually or mentally."

The light changed on Broadway, and the street sounds rushed around us as the camera crew tried to walk ahead. Being New Yorkers, none of the passersby took any notice. I observed, "You're a very private person, you just go from your home down to the Met and back again. You don't seem to go in between."

"That's true," she said. "When I go down to the Met, I just can't sort of wander. I've got to get out of New York to do my wandering. I've got to go to India or Holland to wander."

As for the so-called glamor of the opera star, I asked why she avoided parties and social occasions.

She smiled. "Unless I'm giving them. I give one or two parties a year. I never go to parties. I'm not very social, I suppose."

I could see that a casual conversation on the street, as she raced to rehearsal, was no time to try and dig deep. Besides, the crew was gasping for breath.

Before she disappeared into the revolving door at the Met, Teresa laughed, "I think I've never walked this slowly in my life." And she was gone.

So we filmed the late afternoon light on the exterior of the Met. I had come to know the building quite well some years earlier, while making my film *Homage to Chagall—The Colours of Love.* In the days that followed I would have a great deal of time to study the splendid Chagall works that dominate the great modern square. The murals

With Franco Zeffirelli and the author, 1981.

must be the most widely seen works of modern art in the world. Over four million people every year attend various theaters in Lincoln Center. I recalled Chagall saying, "On these walls are to be found the heroes of music; the singers and dancers who have wanted and who yearn to play the contents of the dream of their lives for all of us." It warmed me that frosty November evening to think of Chagall because of the complex problems I'd had in finally convincing him to pose for his film portrait, a film that became the most-seen art documentary in all of history. And somehow it pleased me to think that now, inside the Met, Teresa was one of those singing "the contents of the dream" of *her* life, while we were parked outside.

Each day of the week brought a new delay. By now we had seen sunrises and sunsets on the Met. We'd filmed the organized chaos of the lobby of her building, outside of which I placed my calls from a pay-phone on Broadway. It became a kind of exterior office—we must have looked like a portable bookie joint. The crew waited patiently, and I waited on air, flying about on faith like a sheep in Chagall blue.

Finally it was agreed that Saturday would be the day. But Saturday, when I called from my Bell outpost, a very weak-sounding Teresa answered the phone. "Leave the crew behind and come up with Aili." Aili Suurallik was my script assistant, a young woman of cheer and patience, with an extra dimension of compassion.

The door of the apartment was already open. "Come in," a faint voice called.

We found Teresa stretched out on the hardwood floor of her bedroom. "Shall I get a doctor?" I inquired.

"No," she said, "I was up all night with Lenya. They kept the temperature almost at freezing to help her breathe. Now my back's stiff and my neck is aching and I can't stand." Each phrase was accompanied by hard breathing. "I've sent for Mano," she whispered. (Mano Mathews, her gentle, helpful nephew, is a massage therapist.)

"Leave Aili behind. She can make some tea."

And so I was banished to wait and see if Teresa could perform.

At one o'clock I returned. Teresa seemed worse than ever, and I made a decision. I called in through the open door and asked Aili to advise Teresa that I had decided to go to the opera. I had never seen *The Magic Flute* with Chagall's sets, and it was being performed that afternoon. Would Teresa arrange for a ticket, the opera being, as usual, sold out? With the phone on the floor, Teresa called through and one ticket was arranged.

It was a gamble.

I stood in the back of the dress circle and tried to hear the opera. Tamino seemed to understand my plight: "Help me; oh, help me! or I am lost, condemned as sacrifice to the cunning serpent!"

The complex and magnificent opera wound its melodic way through the afternoon as I kept dwelling on my last instructions to my excellent cameraman, Ken Gregg: "At four o'clock you enter Teresa's apartment and set up the lights at the pre-arranged spot at her couch. I won't be there. I'll come by when the opera is over."

I kept checking my watch, anxious to leave, but somehow feeling there is a symmetry to all things. I needed to see the opera through until the right triumphs, Tamino and Pamina are united, and Papageno joins his promised love.

I didn't stay for the well-deserved curtain calls, but raced down through the Met's elegant lobby. Striding up Broadway, I had trouble breathing as I tried not to look like a thief on the lam. The short blocks seemed endless.

The lobby was deserted. No sign of the crew. Had they packed up and left for home? The elevator chugged up to Teresa's floor. I knocked nervously.

An effervescent Teresa flung the door open wide, greeting me with a smile that spread across her beautiful, expressive face. "Why Harry, I never thought you'd stay for the whole opera. We've been waiting for you."

And so they were. The camera was loaded. The lights set. And we were to begin.

Now there was eagerness and electricity in the air. None of us present that evening would ever witness anything like it again.

My transcript records the first question: "Okay? Well, Teresa. I don't believe it. Here we are. Let's do it chronologically if we can. Because everybody's life is chronological, at the same time as it has many layers. Going back to the circumstances of your birth . . . where was it specifically? And your memory of just the early days. . . ."

Act One

The curtain rises slowly on the first set: Toronto, 1938. That background played a dominant role in Teresa's life, as it did for the children of immigrants from any non-British land. No one who did not live through that time can know how foreign Toronto then was for a foreigner.

The city of half a million or so was eighty-percent British and Protestant and proud of its narrow view of the world. One of the biggest days of the year was simply called "the Twelf." Even foreigners were supposed to know about July 12 and the 1690 Battle of the Boyne, when Prince William of Orange defeated his Catholic father-in-law, James II, and assured Protestant succession to the British throne. (No one mentioned that William was a Dutchman and therefore a foreigner.) The festivities, led by the mayor with top hat and orange sash, on a horse if possible, were attended by most of the city council and board of education, numerous members of Parliament, and officials ranging from the city architect to the chairman of the parking authority and the municipal abattoir commissioner. Their goal was clearly stated: "the promotion and propagation of True Protestantism" and a defense against any attempt to undercut the monarchy. Such bigotry was only one facet of a mean-spiritedness that left its mark on every aspect of life in Toronto. The swings in public parks were padlocked nightly, and during the heat wave of 1936, thirty men were arrested at the Sunnyside free beach and charged with indecent exposure—they had dared to appear in public wearing only swimming trunks, which revealed bare chests. It was no accident that two of Toronto's most popular mayors were undertakers.

Ten years of the Great Depression had only heightened Toronto's traditional xenophobia. At school, when children were asked to name "the three great races that made Canada," the expected answer was "the English, the Irish, and the Scots." The Jewish population was

"This artist is an elemental force, and to listen to her has never been safe"— High Fidelity, *1987.*

small—Canada as a whole had the worst record of any western nation for accepting Jewish immigrants before World War II—and the black community even smaller. Here and there could be found a Chinese hand-laundry, but it was almost invariably run by a bachelor; Chinese women and children were a rare sight. And if Torontonians were acquainted with anyone from Greece, it was probably the proprietor of the local greasy-spoon, who, whatever his name, would always be known as Nick.

Enter Teresa. "I was born in a building on the corner of Dundas Street and George Street, just above a Chinese laundry. I don't think it exists anymore. May 26, 1938, born on my parents' dining-room table. Delivered by a drunken Irish doctor—when I was causing some kind of a problem my mother would say 'Ah, that doctor, he must have dropped you on your head!' I obviously don't have memories there. Then we moved to 314 Dundas Street East. I remember steps going up, very abruptly. At the top was a flat, and we lived in there. I have a lot of memories from there—I was the youngest one and we all used to run to the ice truck when it would come. The older of the mob of children that lived in the neighborhood would climb up onto the truck and get little pieces of ice. No, I wasn't the youngest, as a matter of fact. There was one child younger than me and she had wandered out behind the truck. The truck backed up to drive away and the child was killed. I remember that very specifically because I was not allowed to go out to play anymore. I had to stand on the other side of the glass door and look out onto Dundas Street. There was a little area on the inside of the door and the door had a glass, and I could just barely see above it. It was an immigrant area. It was a poor area. At that time you didn't know you were poor. You know, you lived and you laughed and you cried and you did whatever any other children did. I think I was too young to know very much then. I didn't really know we were poor."

In 1936 the most exciting story in the local papers had been the last gun battle of Red Ryan, a Toronto gangster who was a kind of folk hero. That same year the *Star* had headlined the Moose River mine disaster—other people's sorrow was big news. By 1939 the Dionne quintuplets were five years old and attracting the kind of world fame to Callender, Ontario, that had been reserved for Niagara Falls. When Their Majesties George V and Elizabeth came to Toronto on a royal tour in the same year, the king looked just like a king was supposed to look, and the regal Elizabeth seemed to be corseted permanently. If the infant Teresa had been near a radio she might have heard the theme music from Al Leary's nightly sportscast on

Argero and Emmanuel Stratas.

CKCL, "Smoke Gets in Your Eyes," played on a harmonica.

As Teresa talked, she seemed to be seeing herself in those days. "I'm told that around the time of my birth my dad was working at a place on Yonge Street called the Harmony Lunch or Harmony Grill—something like that. And he lost his job. I think a lot of people were being laid off at that time, not only at the Harmony Grill, but in Toronto in general. It was obviously a great crisis. Both my father and mother barely spoke English, and they had three children. You can imagine, back then, losing your job—how devastating such a thing would be."

If a man was lucky enough to have a job, chances were that he was in the civil service. The average yearly salary was around $900. The Depression lasted longer in Canada than in the U.S., and with it the prejudice was more powerful, making it almost impossible for most immigrants to find anyone to hire them. They had to barter and borrow and somehow try to start up their own business. That was how Teresa moved early on to a smaller town, just outside Toronto, where she registered for public school.

"My family had scraped enough money together to buy a little restaurant called the Victory Lunch, on King Street, in Oshawa."

A photograph from that time shows a smiling young girl staring into the camera with her protective mother beside her, both wearing their best. But even then there is a sad, adult look to the child.

In the course of our conversation I asked her about it: "In one of your interviews you said when you were ten years old you felt you were a hundred. What did you mean by that?"

Teresa clung to a bright silk pillow and drew a deep breath. "Well, I think it was because of the circumstances of growing up in an immigrant atmosphere. Very very Greek, hanging onto the Greek traditions, because that's all they had to hang onto. The Greeks—especially the Cretans—tend to live a whole lifetime of emotions in each day. I mean, each day you've had your tragedy, you've had your big comic relief—you've gone the whole gamut of emotions in one day. And we did this all the time. It was a way of life."

I couldn't help thinking of the extraordinary day that had begun with Teresa flat on her back, unable to function. Now here was this vibrantly expressive, articulate person reaching forcefully back into her past. I said, "Even today I think we went through a little bit of that. And I wonder whether you feel that other people should do it too. Are they supposed to have their ups so high ... and their tragic—"

She interrupted my question to shake her head. "I don't think so. It's a very intense way of living. I don't know if I recommend it. You know, it was a terrible way of living and it was a wonderful way of living! I have the most incredible happy memories ... and on the other hand I have memories that are—I can't talk about them—they're so horrific ... "

She rearranged herself on the couch. "I think I've gone through most of my life trying to find an equilibrium, trying to find some kind of balance. The great thing in Greek writing is to find the balance. All the great writers, the Greek writers and philosophers, said that the key to life is finding the balance—between the light and the dark—and not being an extreme." She moved her slender arms as if attempting to balance the scales of justice or wisdom, shrugged and smiled: "Unfortunately I still haven't found the balance."

During the interview in StrataSphere.

She dropped the pillow and eased back on the couch, ready for a change of topic. All the reading I had done about her emphasized the warm and loving woman who was her mother. "Your mother seemed to be a woman of terrific fullness. Can we talk a little about her? How would you describe her?"

To my surprise, she replied, "May we talk about my father first?"

I'd read that her father had angrily resented her birth because it meant another mouth to feed, and that when she was a child he sometimes hurled her across the room. She had told *The New Yorker*: "People often say to me, 'You move so beautifully on the stage. Were you ever a dancer?' I don't tell them, but I learned to move by dodging my father when he grabbed for me around the dining-room table." According to the article he suffered from a manic-depressive psychosis. Teresa told the interviewer: "Obviously, he couldn't help that he had this illness. As far as work was concerned, he fluctuated between the point where he was not working at all and a state of euphoria in which he thought he could conquer the world—and that was much harder to handle, of course. During his manic phases, he drank. Drinking is one of the small things they do in that ghastly state—things that have left their mark on me. Not that I think manic depressive psychosis is hereditary. But my childhood was spent in a state of panic. Half the year, we were dodging a killer maniac; the other half, we were trying to keep him from killing himself."

And so I urged her on. "Yes. How about your father, who is very complex, I think?"

She was serious and seeming to want to forgive, to understand, even to justify. "I think whatever talent I might have I get from my father. When he left Crete, he didn't have a pair of shoes. He used to go barefoot up and down the hills of Crete. And to leave Crete, to go away and find a better life, he borrowed—he took his dead brother's boots and wore those. A number of sizes too big. Well, he came from a very very little village that today still doesn't have electricity. To get there—it's very steep—the only way is to get on a donkey, and you have to keep going sideways to get up to the top. It's called 'Stratiana,' which means Stratasville. My father had very little education, almost none. He arrived with the clothes on his back and was suddenly thrown into another, a whole different world at a very young age. He was in his teens. When I think of him leaving Crete with his brother's boots on and going to Canada and raising his family, I really am filled with admiration. Because I don't know how he did it. I don't know how he did it and survived at all. To take that one step further, when I think that my father was in the mountains of Crete in those circumstances and how I, not that many years later, am singing on all the great operatic stages of the world, the Metropolitan Opera, etcetera, etcetera ... that's very hard sometimes—all the time—to justify in my mind, because it's such an extreme."

Whenever an artist emerges in a family that does not seem to have a predisposition to talent, it's natural to look for the source. There are the prodigies who suddenly reach up to a piano and play Mozart even before they can read. I had already gone to see Dr. L.G. Polymenakos, a kind of elder statesman—doctor, judge, counsellor, wise-man-at-large, boss—of the Greek community in Toronto. Because he was a physician, he knew all the immigrant Greeks. They came to him not only with pain, seeking help, but for a contact with the hostile city around them. When he arrived at the end of World War II there were only fifteen hundred people of Greek heritage in the city. He knew everyone.

"Yes, I knew the family. I knew Teresa as a child. She was always a vivacious girl. She sang at our fairs, sang our patriotic songs. She copied the style of a Greek lady who was singing during the war, Sophia Vembo. She wanted to sing continuously."

I asked if he had had any idea that Teresa would become a superstar.

Polymenakos replied without hesitation. "The mother was very dominant. She had the feeling for Teresa, that she would become a great artist. And she called me one day—I remember it very well—and she said to me that when Teresa accomplishes her studies, one day she will be in the Metropolitan Opera. The mother predicted it." According to Dr. Polymenakos, Mrs. Stratas made her prediction before Teresa had even heard an opera. "Even as a child she had this total presence . . . even as a child."

And where did it come from?

"I tell you, I believe it's a chromosome, something, from the history of Crete. Because the family had no tradition of any music, you know. But she is the descendant of a civilization of three thousand years, and so one of the chromosomes came up in Teresa, that's my simple explanation. You see, there is a kind of heredity there. I don't believe this voice just came from nothing."

I wanted to find out more about Teresa's father. When I spoke to Dr. Polymenakos, he said, "I don't believe the father had anything to do with the education of the child, because, first of all, he had some problems, but the mother was behind the girl all the time. I knew them well and I'm sure about that. That's the fact . . . the influence was from the mother, and she's a product of her mother."

Mrs. Stratas was, in fact, the classic immigrant mother. She was the keeper of the home, nourisher of the children, never stopping to consider her personal needs. The object was to save the future through the children.

Teresa on the subject of her mother is all enthusiasm. Her eyes glow with memory: "My mother was brought over by her brothers to come to the United States. They had done what we call a *proxenia*. They had found her a groom and were going to marry her off. They happened to know my father's brothers, who brought him over, and asked if they would mind if my mother came and stayed in their home until they could bring her into the United States. They agreed, and my mother arrived in Canada to total strangers and was staying in the home of my father's brother. You know all Greek stories sound like that—my father's brother's uncle, sister—because everyone's related. So she was staying with my father's brother and his wife and this man that was supposed to marry her came to Canada and saw her. He was an old man, very very old, and my mother was extremely young, in her teens. On top of that, as the story goes, he was a vegetarian and he was saying, 'In my house you can't eat meat,' and this was this—he was laying down the rules. He left that evening and went to his hotel room and my mother cried and cried. And my father said 'Don't worry, I'll marry you. We'll go away. I love you.' "

I asked Teresa, "Was there music in the house?"

She seemed to hear the sounds. "Oh yes. Oh my goodness yes. There was a lot of music in the house. The Greeks sing and dance a lot and break plates. All those things that one hears about the Greeks, they're all true. We do break plates. But it isn't always so wonderful, like in *Zorba the Greek*, when everybody's smiling, breaking the plates. Sometimes at the end of a heated evening of dance and song one is breaking things for other reasons. It's that whatever frustrations one has danced out or sung out, or whatever happiness one is expressing, sometimes goes to a higher pitch.

"The Cretans have songs that are typical only of Crete—and there, you see, I come from a house of music and poetry—because the Cretans' songs are couplets, beautiful poetry set to a certain melodic line. They're called *mandinades* and they're made up. One person sits there and makes up the poetry and the other people in the room, the relatives and the friends, repeat the line. I'll give you an example. It's typical only of Crete and you must remember that from the time I was very very little I was brought up on this kind of poetry, or this kind of music. I have to think, think back ... "

She sang:

"Poté sou min xehnás ta próta scalopátia.

And then everyone says:

Éla éla ta próta scalopátia,
Yiati s'aftá protopatís ke bénis sta palátia,
Yiati s'aftá protopatís ke bénis sta palátia,
éla éla ke bénis sta palátia.

It goes on and on and then the next person will continue on from there, perhaps taking that theme and giving an answer and saying 'ah but ...' "

I asked, "What does that mean?"

"That means—it's very hard to translate, because there are many meanings to some of the words. '*Poté sou min xehnás ta próta scalopátia*': 'Don't ever forget your first steps'; *Yiati s'aftá protopatís*': 'Because on those first steps you walk'; '*Ke bénis sta palátia*': 'and enter into your castles, paradises or goals.' In other words, don't forget your origins because they're your foundations and they're leading you to the better. But I can't really translate it. It's beautiful poetry. Oh, they had a lot of history. They touched on different themes—it may be love, hate, revenge, death. And then of course we danced a lot. We did the Cretan dances and the Greek dances. Part of our life centered around what was happening at the Greek community and we were also active members of what was happening. We children went to Sunday school, and to Greek school in the evenings, and my mother was a member of the Philoptoxos, which was the ladies' organization. We went to the Greek dances and marched in the Greek parades. I made my first appearances singing at all those Greek functions. I remember—it's very interesting—right from the beginning it always was hell to get up and perform in front of an audience. I remember, even as a small child, if we went to someone's home, being absolutely terrified all evening. All that loomed in my mind was, Ah, someone might ask me to sing. And I would sit there and prepare myself the whole evening in case someone asked me. Sure enough, I was usually asked to sing, and I was always relieved that people enjoyed it."

The Toronto of those years was decorated in gray sludge. Homes were heated by coal, frequently coal stoves in the kitchen. The ashes were saved to throw on the ice outdoors, like salt, to melt it. When the snow and ice and ashes congealed, it made a kind of snow soup. The city was a visual dirge, and its suffocating air helped to bring on an early case of tuberculosis. Teresa nearly died. The doctor recommended a sanatorium, but like many immigrants of the time, the family decided to keep the illness a secret. There was always the fear that somehow they would be returned to the poverty they had escaped in the old world. Disease had to be kept hidden, otherwise the other children might be kept out of school; perhaps the police would even come and deport the whole family. If Teresa was to survive she would have to fight it out. And fight she did. She recovered, but there is still a scar on her left lung that acts up when she overworks. With someone as driven as Teresa, it happens often.

But there was at least one time when the fight was too much. Life was too hostile. She felt like an intruder. When she saw the bills arrive and the tears in her mother's eyes, she decided that perhaps the family had one too many members to support. She took sleeping pills, locked herself in the bathroom, and slashed her wrists with a razor. As she told the story to *The New Yorker*: "I wanted to make one less problem for my mother. It was very interesting. I suppose I was in another dimension because of the pills. Everything seemed to be in slow motion. I sat on the edge of the bathtub and watched myself. At some point, I must have fallen to the floor. My brother heard the fall and broke down the door. My parents' reaction was like their reaction to the T.B. It was that no one must find out that I tried to commit suicide." Once again the immigrants feared the authority of the police. "They didn't want me to go to the doctor. But my brother yelled, 'If we don't get her to the emergency room, she is going to die!' And then I remember that I couldn't quite comprehend that I might die. They carried me down, put me in a car, and took me to the emergency room, where I got fifteen stitches in one wrist and ten in the other. There was just an intern there, and he sewed me up without anesthetic or anything. But I remember I felt no pain."

I asked, "Why did you do that?"

"Well, as I said before, we lived a whole lifetime each day. Everything was to the extreme. Whatever the problem was, it was to the extreme. If we couldn't pay our bills ... Greeks are very proud people. I remember my mother sitting in the kitchen crying over the bills night after night. I guess at some romantic young foolish age I thought maybe if she had one less mouth to feed ... but that's not the way it worked." She paused and then added, with a smile, "Fate had it I would stay on."

"But you seemed fascinated by death. Is that because of the Greek heritage?"

"It could be. I don't know. I don't know that 'fascinated' is the right word. Certainly I'm more accepting of it than most people. Most people don't want to know about it, or pretend it's not there, or that it happens to everybody else and doesn't happen to them. I think at this point in my life I'm wise enough to know that I shouldn't push it. I mean I should really try to hang in there until fate has it that it's time to go. However, when it's time to go, I certainly do welcome it. I think I see it as a release or a freedom of some kind, I think that's the ultimate freedom."

Growing up during the Depression cast a pall over Teresa's childhood. The times demanded a practical use of all things—wrappings for Sunkist oranges became rough toilet paper; orange crates served as extra items of furniture; and the sturdy sacks for Primrose Flour doubled as undershirts. In light of today's trendy message T-shirts, Teresa manages to laugh: "You know it was a time of being frugal. My mother used to make bed linen out of the flour sacks, pillow cases ... I had a little inside shirt that said 'Primrose Flour' across my chest—I used to hate taking my clothes off for gym. I had this shirt that said 'Primrose Flour.' Today it would be very fashionable, of course. My mother was very incredible. Everybody thinks their

The Stratas family around 1940: left to right in the first row, Nicholas, Teresa and Mary.

mother was incredible, but my mother really was incredible. She was a great lady."

I asked, "What was her greatest gift to you, do you think?"

"I have my talent from my father, but anything I might have accomplished in my life, I have my mother to thank for it. She was highly ambitious for her children. Now one reads all the time in the paper about women with the difficulty of raising a family and having a job also. But my mother did it back then. She ran the house. She organized us for school. She washed our clothes—in those days they

*In front of the Victory
Lunch, wearing her
first brand-new coat
and hat.*

used scrub boards—and she worked in the restaurant day and night
and in between. She worked all hours. I don't ever remember her
going to sleep and I don't remember her sitting down and eating a
complete meal and not saying, 'Oh, I feel full—why don't you have
the rest?'

"I remember a conversation when I was in the restaurant helping
my mother and one of these Greek ladies came in and said to my
mother—and I think they were talking about my brother Nick at
the time—he's old enough to stop going to school and he could help
in the restaurant—and look at you—look how you dress—you don't
have anything. You don't have any jewelry, etcetera, etcetera. My
mother said, 'My children are my jewelry.'"

Out of these early experiences Teresa has drawn a kind of inner
philosophy. "No, I would not have done what I have done and led
the life I did had I not come from a background of poverty. I wouldn't
be where I am now—wherever that is—had I been born into a middle-
class Canadian family. When you're terribly aware of the lack of
things—though we had everything that counted in our family—well,
you're goaded into going the distance. One more than compensates
to make up the void of knowledge that begins and ends at oneself."

Somehow the family that had nothing found a way of possessing
an instrument of escape—a piano. The story materialized when I
asked her if in those early years she'd had any musical training.

"When I was two years old, my sister tells me, my mother and
father somehow scraped together $75, which was a lot of money in
those days, to buy a piano. And the reason they bought the piano
was that my sister had been crying and crying that she wanted to be

a dancer, wanted dancing lessons. Now Mary at that time—if I was two, she was seven. We were living on Dundas Street, and because we lived up at the top of the flight of stairs, there were people, obviously, that lived downstairs. So she had only one lesson. My sister never became the dancer she wanted to become, but to compensate, my mother and father bought this piano. And as my sister tells me, much to her frustration, a piano teacher used to come to the house and then she'd spend all week trying to learn that tune. But as soon as that teacher would leave, having shown her the new song—I was two years old, I don't remember it, my sister tells me this—I would walk over to the piano and play whatever it was. She'd feel like murdering me, of course. So this is what happened after each piano lesson. I obviously had an ear for picking out tunes."

"But a piano was an incredible investment for a family that was having trouble," I suggested.

"Absolutely. We were a family of extremes."

Her parents had scraped up enough money to open what might be described as a "greasy spoon," a place with a fine odor of reused olive oil and burnt coffee grounds.

"I lived in a dream world. My mother worked and had no time for me, so she put me in movie houses every day with a sandwich in a paper bag. I saw every movie over and over. It was a world of make-believe and I loved it. I sang from as early as I can remember, and I learned to play the piano really well by ear. Sometime I had the hell beaten out of me, but there was also a lot of loving in our family." At the age of four, she sang to her pet cat and one day she sang to some animals she found in the basement of her home: "When my mother found me she beat me and cried at the same time. I was singing to sewer rats." Teresa's first song was "Pistol-Packin' Mama," which at the age of five she sang for the customers in the family restaurant. They threw nickels and dimes to her.

After several years in Oshawa, the Stratas family decided to resettle in Toronto, where there was a larger Greek community, a Greek church, and the opportunities of a big city. The Stratas family moved often. While they were living in the working-class area of Main and Danforth, in the east end, the children attended Malvern Collegiate. Interestingly, the same school produced another international musical celebrity, Glenn Gould.

In her final years at school Teresa decided to quit because she had begun to do well at her singing career. She sang in the Toronto movie houses, when there used to be live entertainment; she sang on the radio; she sang torch songs at places like the Mercury Club. Describing those days in a *Maclean's* interview, she said, "I had to keep the attention of all the drunks—an experience that pays off when I sing to the sometimes dozing opera audiences who come to listen for social reasons."

On her sixteenth birthday fate showed itself in the true Dickensian tradition of the multiple coincidence. A drunk came into the Stratas' family restaurant and somehow mislaid his wallet. After eating he paid for his meal with two tickets to the Metropolitan Opera, which was on tour in Toronto.

Mrs. Stratas gave the tickets to Teresa and her brother, Nick. Teresa didn't want to go: "I had heard negative things about opera. It was for rich people, and it was sung in a foreign language that I couldn't understand." But Nick insisted. "Then I went, and it changed my life."

The site was Maple Leaf Gardens, the vast arena that former Toronto alderman William Kilbourn has called "the most important religious building in Canada." Though dedicated above all to the national cult of hockey, the Gardens has hosted everything from religious revival meetings to political rallies, from Beatles concerts to the Bolshoi ballet. So it was in that great ungodly cathedral that Teresa discovered opera. The performance was *La Traviata*, with Licia Albanese, Jan Peerce, and Leonard Warren, and Pietro Cimara conducting. (Some interviewers have cited *La Bohème* with Renata Tebaldi as her first opera.) As Teresa recalled that night, she seemed to become a sixteen-year-old again:

"I was overwhelmed. I mean there was this wonderful story—a sad story, but wonderful. The sets and the costumes and a whole world and a hundred musicians in the pit—to me it looked like hundreds—playing this fabulous music. And the most incredible, extraordinary part of it all, was the people opening their mouths, making incredible sounds come out of the human body. I thought: That's what I want to do. That night really changed the course of my life."

Teresa has always been direct. As soon as she knew she wanted to be an opera singer she simply set about becoming one. She took the street car to the Faculty of Music at the University of Toronto, housed in a Victorian pseudo-castle that would terrify a lesser individual. She found a cold reception from the British-sounding secretary in an outer office, who smiled sarcastically at the explosive teenager announcing her ambitions for the musical world: "What, you have no accompanist?" The woman all but condemned Teresa to leave. But she would not go until she sang for someone. One of the students waiting offered to play for her.

She was escorted into the study of Dr. Arnold Walter, founder of the Opera School at the Royal Conservatory of Music and head of the Faculty of Music. The shelves were lined with leather-bound books, books of music, librettos. She had no aria or lied to perform— she didn't know what they were. So she sang the only song she thought might impress, Jerome Kern's "Smoke Gets in Your Eyes." Dr. Walter listened first with amusement, and then seriously. He would have a profound effect on her life.

"I had a natural voice," Teresa told me. "The person who thought it was special right from the beginning was Dr. Walter. He was a wonderful man, who has now passed away." Walter maintained his interest in Teresa, spending time with her during lunch hours, showing her art books in his office, telling her about great literature, introducing her to the world of culture and art. "I don't know how he ever realized that there was a special talent there. But he gave me a scholarship and sent me to Irene Jessner ... and I started studying."

The meeting with former Metropolitan Opera singer Irene Jessner was a happy one, and it began a relationship that continues today. A prominent soprano before she turned to teaching, known especially for her performances of the Marschallin in Strauss's *Der Rosenkavalier*, Madame Jessner still observes, if from a distance, every move. "Irene Jessner was my first and only singing teacher, thank heavens. Because the one thing she taught me, the most important thing, was that singing was a natural thing, and that you mustn't do anything unnatural. You know when I came to New York ... everyone has a method: 'What technique does your teacher teach?' This one teaches to breathe with this muscle back here and this one teaches by telling their pupils to smell a rose and some people stick a pencil in their mouth and all kinds of weird things. She taught me to sing naturally, and for that I truly thank her."

Sitting at a grand piano in her Toronto studio, in grand style, Madame Jessner recalls Teresa. Her voice, accented equally with Europe and music, makes every statement she utters sound like part of an important aria: "I was very impressed with her voice, the quality of the voice. She had a very dark timbre. She sang like somebody sings who never had any lessons, and she never studied before. And when she came to me she didn't know anything classical, she sang something like 'Smoke Gets in Your Eyes.' Then she was accepted in the Faculty of Music. And when she started to sing with the right technique she improved tremendously. Very soon she went into opera school—Mr. Herman Geiger-Torel, who was then the director

With conductor Walter Susskind and Irene Jessner, after singing Mimi with the Canadian Opera Company, 1958.

of the Canadian Opera Company, was also the director of the opera school. And one day he told me: 'I can't teach her anything. She's so talented, she goes on stage and just does it, instinctively the right thing.' He never had to tell her anything."

I asked, "What is it that makes the difference between a singer and a great singer? What is the difference?"

To Madame Jessner it was clear: "She had an instinct for singing. She had an instinct for expression, for emotion. You know when she sang something she was always very emotional, sometimes too emotional. I remember we had a performance of *Bohème*. In the third act, in the scene between Rodolfo and Marcello, there is a duet, and she was hiding in the back, listening. And when she heard that she was so sick, she started to cry. And when she came on and sang you could hear that she cried. She was very emotional."

"Were you surprised when she became a Metropolitan singer?"

Her answer was immediate. "I was not surprised, because she sang so beautifully. She won the Metropolitan auditions—she was really ready for it. She sang, and it was so beautiful. I was not surprised because everything was there—the talent, the voice, the musicality. She is tremendously musical. She learns things in no time. I remember when she was still at the Faculty of Music she had, sometimes, the opportunity to sing little concerts, and one day she was flying somewhere and she learned the song in the plane. She just looked at it and knew it, learned very quick. And she's a perfectionist, an absolute perfectionist. Something has to be absolutely one hundred percent. Otherwise she doesn't do it."

When I asked Teresa about this quest for perfection, she spoke of positive and negative energy. "I might very well be mad if I didn't have that place to channel all that energy. It's obviously a lot of energy being brought together, but it's totally consuming in that moment, so I can't tell you what I feel. It's such a total concentration, it's the only time, almost the only time in my life, I can say that for a complete period of time no other thoughts enter my mind. I'm not worried about anything.

"The only time I really and truly look in the mirror is when I'm sitting there very coldly, very professionally, putting on my makeup before a performance. Other than that I sort of cringe when I'm passing a mirror and catch sight of myself. Maybe it's because I have become so many people. When does one stop being Stratas and become Lulu, or Salome? Where do you draw the lines? And aren't I, when I'm doing the role of Lulu, really drawing upon my own self to portray that? On the other hand, when I'm not working, and I don't have a mask or a skin to put on, I no longer know who I am. It's very . . . it's sometimes . . . it's been dangerous.

"I mean sometimes when I look in the mirror in the morning, I have a total loss of identity. Because who am I? Am I the daughter of the man from the island of Crete or am I the one that was born in Toronto, going to school and learning and—who was it that we learned about? I couldn't identify with them at all, the one that Mary played ball with . . . Mary and—who were they in our school, Mary and Jane? No, Jane, Dick and Jane. Dick and Jane could've been from Mars or I could've been from Mars. I mean I just didn't identify with Dick and Jane and their parents at all."

Act Two

The curtain rises on the brilliant skyline of New York City. The time is the late fifties and Manhattan is the dream landscape that every poor kid with ambition aspires to conquer.

At the gates of the metropolis arrive two women: the determined immigrant mother and the teenager who heard her first opera only three years before, at Maple Leaf Gardens. And conquer they do. At nineteen Teresa walks onto the stage of the Metropolitan Opera for the Metropolitan Opera Auditions of the Air (broadcast by ABC radio). She wins a contract, and is soon singing at the Met.

"Bing was crazy about her from the beginning," Irene Jessner recalls. Sir Rudolf (he was knighted in 1971) considered Teresa one of his finest discoveries : "Many talented singers could not start at the Met. They had to launch their careers in various European houses. But Teresa Stratas came to the Met as an audition winner. She is an uncommon talent and personality with a lovely voice." For his *New Yorker* portrait, Winthrop Sargeant interviewed Bing, who recalled the audition: "She has a beautiful voice. But what struck me at the audition was the way she looked. This was a fascinating personality. You knew that the person onstage was somebody."

The old Metropolitan Opera House, on Broadway between 39th and 40th Streets, was a kind of castle without turrets. It should have terrified anyone setting foot on its enormous stage for the first time, but for Teresa the size and grandeur were somehow balanced by the vastness of her mother's confidence. Asked if she recalled her first steps onto the stage of opera history, she said no: "I don't remember anything about that period. I was so supported by my mother—knowing I could do anything—that she brainwashed me. I didn't stop and think, 'What am I doing singing at the Metropolitan Opera?' for as long as she lived. It was after she died that the rug was really pulled out from under my feet and I thought, oh my God, who am I—this little Greek girl from uneducated origins—what am I doing in this

As Nedda in a Munich production of Pagliacci, *1978. "Like all great performers, she has an alluring sexual ambiguity"*—The New Statesman.

With her parents on the stage of the Metropolitan Opera, immediately after winning a contract in the 1959 audition.

city? They're going to find me out. They're going to find out that I'm really bluffing and I don't know anything about opera or music or art ... "

The voice trails off. The facts are not quite like that. Teresa knows a great deal. She reads—in half a dozen languages. She thinks. Unlike many performers, who see nothing beyond the confines of their own parts, Teresa knows the whole universe around each of her characters. She seems to plunge deep into the composer's heart.

She made her Metropolitan debut in 1959 in the small role of Poussette in Massenet's *Manon*. She brought her parents to live in New York, and later her father would sometimes turn up backstage in one of his manic periods, demanding to see her. Teresa lived in fear of these spells, and sometimes Bing would step in himself to divert Mr. Stratas. Bing was an understanding adviser. After her mother's death, Teresa began to suffer bouts of stagefright, and he reassured her by explaining that other performers had similar problems.

Despite his experience as a nurse to temperament, however, Bing found Teresa special. It would have been normal to go on playing *comprimario* parts for half a dozen years. But that was not Teresa's style. She confessed to a *New York Times* reporter: "My first year at the Met was a great experience . . . but I had enough of that. I needed to do something else. I was not happy, and I asked to be let out of my contract. And then I stepped in as Liu in *Turandot* when Lucine Amara was ill."

Critics and audience united to rejoice at the dazzling new talent singing with Birgit Nilsson and Franco Corelli that night in 1961. She had never had a stage and orchestra rehearsal for the part, and her costume was pinned together. No matter. She was a star. One reviewer, Alan Rich, said of her performance: "Not only did she sing her music with beautiful tenderness, but also she was always a pleasure to watch. One of Liu's great problems is what to do during the long periods when she is on stage but not singing. Miss Stratas seemed at all times to be a part of the drama." The *New York Herald Tribune* of March 10, 1961 concluded its praise: "She revealed a voice of liquid purity capable of producing a beautifully sustained legato phrase and remarkably well controlled crescendos. It is to be hoped that she will be given further significant roles before the season's end."

But success can have a terrible side. As Rudolf Bing observed, opera singers have a strange situation in life—"If they are great artists, they wake up one day to find themselves catapulted into enormous fame and riches. They have cover pictures in *Time* and *Newsweek*, their telephone never stops, they race from Vienna to Covent Gardens to Milan to the Metropolitan, they have dinner at the White House, their income rises to $500,000 a year or even more. And for most, this apotheosis follows immediately upon almost total obscurity."

Teresa has thought a lot about the surge of fame. She told Ulla Colgrass of *Music Magazine*: "I was singing at the Met at the age of nineteen. How much faster could I have gone? If you had taken me out of my background and put me elsewhere, I wouldn't be me. Whatever person I am, it's because we had a difficult life. Therefore, if I am sitting here in a fancy, enormous apartment in New York, with Lincoln Center down the street . . . it doesn't mean a thing, because that's not really what life is about. Because of my background I know that those material things are not really very important. I came from this very poor background, and certainly there was a conflict, suddenly finding myself in the glitter and glamor when I first came to the Met. I wasn't sure what was happening to me. But I did sort it out, thanks to my background."

With John Dehner in
The Canadians, *1961.*

*In Athens for the title
role in* Nausicaa,
1960 (left).

It was not long before Hollywood was trying to shape her to its image. She appeared in a 20th Century Fox film called *The Canadians*, playing a captive of the Sioux. Her voice in full flight before a backdrop of splendid mountain scenery, Teresa suggested the mixture of innocence and worldliness she would later perfect. However, as one critic remarked at the time, "A DeMille epic it was not." Teresa was nevertheless offered a three-year studio contract, which she turned down.

The musical world was ready for her to conquer. *Who's Who in America* rhymes off her engagements in those early years: "Appeared as Mimi at Covent Garden-Royal Opera House in London, 1961; appeared with symphony orchestras in Houston, Toronto, Montreal, Ottawa, Detroit; title role world premiere *Nausicaa*, Herod Atticus Theatre, Athens, Greece; appeared as Madame Butterfly, Vancouver International Festival, 1960; operatic debut in *Atlantida*, La Scala Opera, 1962." Everything seemed possible. Comparisons with Maria

In Moscow for Eugene
Onegin, *1963.*

A curtain call after
Bohème *at the old Met
(right). In 1962* Opera
*called her Mimi one of
the most touching
"since Albanese and
Sayão were in their
prime."*

Callas, the overwhelming diva of the day, were unavoidable—some
of her admirers even called her "Baby Callas."

But the glory of stardom was accompanied by the anguish of her
mother's sudden death, in 1963, at the age of fifty-two. "She was my
best friend," Teresa told Emily Coleman of *The New York Times*.
"She traveled with me and she was my backbone." The loss of that
maternal support was devastating, but Teresa found solace in her
music. And, as she explained, at the time her mother died she had
come to "a very frustrating period": "I was singing to go up the
ladder, not to enjoy the work. I was singing to make a career, not to
make music. At twenty-two or twenty-three, I had two or three mink
coats. I was singing everything, everywhere, but I didn't know where
I was going. I was looking for something, but I didn't know what I
was looking for."

The tragedy of her mother's death led to a new understanding:
"I began to see that the scores I had been studying were the same,
the same today as they were yesterday or last week—the same in spite

In costume as Despina, with Rudolf Bing, 1971.

of all the horrible things that had happened in the world of my life in the meantime. They became a security and a comfort, especially after my mother died. Then I came to another terrible period. I would pick up a score and say to myself blankly: 'I can't sing this. What does Puccini want with this dotted sixteenth?' But that uncertainty passed too." Work became a kind of refuge. And Teresa's star continued to rise.

Inevitably, any sign of "temperament" attracted the press. In 1963 Teresa was performing in *Eugene Onegin* at the Bolshoi Theatre in Moscow when she walked out at intermission, feeling she had not received enough applause. What she did not know was that Soviet audiences traditionally wait until the end of a performance to show their appreciation. At a later Bolshoi performance, she received eight curtain calls.

Even more inevitable, perhaps, was the attention drawn by any rumor of romance. On the same trip to Moscow, she met the young conductor Zubin Mehta. Both were dynamic personalities, and soon the press was following them around asking when they would marry. Years later, in his biography *Zubin*, Mehta was quoted as saying: "We never found ourselves with the same day off in the same place at the same time. How could we get married? Besides, Teresa is a confirmed bachelor." The only public comment Teresa made was to *The New York Times*: "Marriage was just not meant for me. It never was one of the big desires of my life . . . About Zubin? Well he, I suppose I can say it, because it's already here in Zubin's biography. He said that we are not together because I'm a confirmed bachelor. I couldn't see myself going through life as Mrs. Conductor. What Zubin needs is someone to take care of him, and that's not me."

An artist's personal relationships should not be public property, and in making the film I tried to avoid prying. Instead, in the course of our conversation I asked Teresa to comment in a more general way: "The character of Salome says at the end that 'love has a bitter taste.' I wonder if that is something you believe yourself. It's Oscar Wilde's line, from the libretto. It's Salome's last exclamation."

Teresa responded with a half-smile: "I don't know, I think I'm tasting it now for the first time in my life. I'll let you know in the future if it had a bitter taste."

The experience she was referring to was her relationship with the English poet Tony Harrison. Known in the opera world as the translator of Smetana's *The Bartered Bride*, in which Teresa starred, he is an extraordinarily talented man who seems as quiet as Teresa is volatile.

Writing in *The New York Post*, Speight Jenkins described her as "a combination of Carmen, Gloria Steinem, and a fresh Juilliard graduate. It isn't just looks, but rather her intense combination of strength and vulnerability. . . . Looking out of deep black eyes, Miss Stratas summed herself up: 'I'm a person who happens to be a woman who happens to be an opera singer. I hate to be categorized or for the character I play to be narrowed down to one dimension.'"

The following photographs show the extraordinary range of Teresa's roles.

As Tatiana in the film of Eugene Onegin, *1971.*

As the Composer in Ariadne auf Naxos, *Munich, 1964. In the* Münchner Abendzeitung *Karl Schumann praised Teresa's "spiritual artistry," and went on to say: "Had Mozart appeared in the delicate figure with the sorrowful glance? Teresa Stratas dares ascend to the utmost heights of expression; she achieved the very limits of theatrical art."*

As Gretel, at the Met, with Rosalind Elias and Karl Dönch, 1967.

As Mařenka in the Met's Bartered Bride, *with Jon Vickers, 1978.*

In the title role of La Périchole *at the Met, with Cyril Ritchard, 1965.*

As Desdemona in the Met's Otello, *1974.*

As Anna Elisa, rehearsing a scene for the film of Paganini, *with Antonio Theba and director Eugen York, 1972.*

As Magda in the CBC-TV *production of* La Rondine, *1970.*

As Sonja in the film of Der Zarewitsch, *with Wieslow Ochman, 1972.*

Two sides of Cherubino in Le Nozze di Figaro. *Of Teresa's Munich performance in 1964, the* Münchner Merkur *observed, "The theater obviously rustled with excitement when she appeared on stage—she played her role with so much fire, charm and tenderness, and with all the magic of youth."*

With Andrea Velis and Judith Raskin in the Met's Nozze di Figaro, *1964.*

As Despina in a Salzburg Cosi fan tutte, *with Tom Krause and Lajos Kozma, 1969.*

In Demented: The World of the Opera Diva, *critic Ethan Mordden has written: "Santuzza is a great role, but her unofficial partner, Nedda, is not—though Nedda is a more intriguing character, with an aria (the Ballatella) unlike anything else in opera and a wonderful last ten minutes in which her professional and private lives collide and shatter onstage during an innocuous comedy. This sort of juxtaposition never fails in theatre; the tension between the foolish farce and the threatening jealous-husband realism (ironically mirrored in the farce) is the very spark of art. The rare soprano who understands this has found much in Nedda—Teresa Stratas, for instance: devastatingly earthy on her entrance, dreamy in the Ballatella, nimbly* dell'arte *in the* commedia. *Still, what star looks forward to a stint as Nedda? Stratas is exceptional; she likes what she likes. Most divas want to like what the public likes."*

As Nedda, with Alberto Rinaldi, in Franco Zeffirelli's film of Pagliacci, *1981.*

As Mélisande in the Met's Pelléas et Mélisande, *with Jerome Hines, 1977.*

Teresa's interpretation of certain roles reveals an astonishing emotional intensity. Most powerful of all was her performance in what may be the greatest opera film ever made: Richard Strauss's *Salome*, directed by Götz Friedrich, with the Vienna Philharmonic conducted by Karl Böhm. Böhm had worked with Strauss, and, according to the *New Yorker* interview, when she rehearsed the role with him, he said: "My child, this is what Strauss had dreamed of but never lived to hear."

The film is extraordinary, and I made as much use of it as I could in *StrataSphere*. Teresa's performance is so powerful that some people have difficulty confronting the passion that projects from the screen. One reason she can achieve such a level of performance may come from her own feelings about the human voice and its possibilities. This is what she told me:

"There's something quite incredible about the human voice—it goes right back to the primal ... Whatever it is we express it with the human voice—anguish, torment, joy, happiness. We laugh, we cry. And opera, when it's done truly well, takes these things which we can't talk about—maybe they're too painful, or it's so much joy that you can't express it—and puts it in a ... Sometimes our pain is so much that if we were to express it we would cry out, and sometimes the emotion is so extreme that no words can contain that emotion, only that primal scream. Only the human voice can truly, truly get to the soul, or to the core of whatever it is that one needs to express. And opera takes this that we can no longer talk about, because it's past talking, and allows us to express it to that nth abstract degree—that emotion that we feel we can't really tell anyone else about. But sometimes you hear a phrase of music that makes you want to weep, because it says it for you."

I asked her another question: "There's such a variety of, if I may say, crazy ladies that you seem to do—I was thinking of the *Salome* production. I don't know how it's possible to portray the violence that you seem to have in that performance. Where do you reach to for that?"

Teresa answered: "I think that we all have the possibility of violence within us. But certainly I saw some degree of violence in my upbringing because of my father's ... because of the problem that our whole family had to deal with and learn to survive. Not only my father but the whole family, because it affects the whole family—manic depression."

Following, a sequence of photographs from the film of Salome.
With Astrid Varnay as Herodias.

When Ulla Colgrass of *Music Magazine* raised the question of temperament, in a long interview, Teresa answered with her usual directness (Colgrass's questions are in italics):

"People often think of opera singers as being essentially temperamental. Is there any truth to that?"

"I know I'm known as being temperamental and difficult, although I don't think I am. I think it has to do with not being comfortable . . . it would have been much easier for me to go through life always agreeing, but I couldn't live with myself that way. If I believe in something, I have to say what it is. If I'm in a room where somebody says something I really disagree with, I'll voice my opinion rather than just be quiet. Maybe that's being difficult. We have gone through life expecting ladies to act like 'ladies', and that usually means not *having* an opinion."

"You are a small person and yet you have a big voice and emit a lot of energy . . ."

"The energy we transmit has nothing to do with the size of the person. It's something from within—well, it's actually from somewhere else. I'm the instrument for transmitting that energy. You can have a great big blubber on stage with absolutely no energy, no waves or electrical force.

"My voice was always enormous. When I was a little child I spoke with this dark, deep voice. In my parents' restaurant in Toronto everybody was shocked at this skinny five-year-old who spoke like an old man. The speaking quality was always this dark, 'resonanty' sound. Sometimes in hotels when I ask for room service over the telephone, they answer 'Yes Sir'! You can imagine that can be very upsetting on the days of a performance. Usually someone my size does the soubrette repertoire and stays in that very light sphere of singing. Certainly my voice was always larger than that."

"Were you ever in danger of being type-cast as the pretty young girl?"

"Never. I started out doing Mimis, Micaelas and Madame Butterfly—already a different kind of repertoire. The people involved with the development of my singing were fortunately highly intelligent and perceptive. They saw the many facets of my personality so that I was never confined by 'Oh, she is a marvelous comedienne, so we will only have her do comic, light parts,' or 'She is a Puccini singer.' No one ever tried to put me in a box and tie a pretty ribbon around it."

"But you must have a favorite repertoire?"

"I must say I don't like that question. I will only do a role when I'm convinced of it. If I'm doing a film of *Salome*, obviously that's

my favorite role at that moment—I lived and ate and breathed that music and those words. If I'm doing *Bohème* I think: what a masterpiece, not one note too many; what a wonderful, vulnerable creature Mimi is. So I can't answer that question."

"*Do you ever tackle a role that's opposite to your natural temperament?*"

"What's natural temperament? I don't think a person has only one temperament. People are not one-dimensional characters. Opera singers are no doubt blessed with more dimensions and I don't say that out of arrogance—we are blessed with that. So I don't think I have ever done a role that has gone against my temperament.

"*In that case, what type of role might you have turned down in the past as being unsuitable?*"

"I took Butterfly out of my repertoire and I'll tell you why. It was very hard for me to be convinced that she couldn't help herself to get out of that situation. There is something a little too passive in her, maudlin and whiny, so it's very hard to be instilling honor, belief and trust and all these other things that one could also interpret in the role. I found I was not convinced, so how could I convince the public? For these reasons I took it out of my repertoire, although it's suited to my voice and I'm always asked to do it."

"*Don't you get to a point when you tire of singing a role again and again and again and want to take a rest from it or abandon it all together?*"

"Well, I'll tell you, as long as what you are doing, you do honestly ...

"I love the camera, I love film and I love television. It gets into your brain and your soul and it says everything that is inside you."

"*You obviously take acting seriously. It would be well if all opera singers did the same.*"

"I never think of one part of it being singing and another part acting. It's all one thing. We are here to give forth emotions, ideas, thoughts. You know, the vocal cords lie in a very strange place, right here in the throat just a little bit above the heart, a little bit above the soul. I sincerely feel that however you are feeling spiritually definitely affects the performance as a whole."

Teresa described the roller-coaster ride of her emotions in an article she wrote herself for a magazine called *Fugue* in March 1979, titled "Thoughts on the Day of a Performance":

"I look at today's newspaper and am confronted with an enormous picture of myself taken during rehearsals, and a fullpage article with a sub-heading that reads "*Wo sie auftaucht, wenn sie nicht gerade absagt, gehen die Uhren anders. Teresa Stratas ist eine Frau mit Ausstrahlung*" (where she appears when she does not cancel, clocks chime differently. Teresa Stratas is a woman who gives off light). And here I sit in a hotel room feeling alone, cold and frightened, beset with the usual self doubts that haunt most artists before a performance. Will I be capable this evening of giving further to my fellow man of that which God has entrusted to me. My gift. My curse? Twenty years of carrying the burden of whichever one it is. And it is a burden that sometimes weighs very heavily. I have sat and laughed and cried with some of my colleagues as we reminisced about times we have stood in traffic hoping that a car would run us down so that we would not have to go to the theater to perform.

"So what is it that drives us on? Why continue such extreme feelings of depression and elation? Yes, the elation does come—a flower from a blind boy who appears at my apartment door in New York to say that my telecast performance of *Pagliacci* (which, remember, he cannot see) has thrilled him and pulled him out of depression. A little girl named Teresa here in Munich. She was named Teresa because her parents had been so moved by my *Traviata* performance here thirteen years ago. I do not know them or Teresa, but I receive pictures and letters of her progress. And suddenly, today, when the phone rings and I answer, I hear a small, sweet and determined voice announce, '*Meine Name ist Teresa.*' My heart does a double flip and I am elated. Yet five minutes later I plunge again into the depths of despair. What am I doing here? Maybe if I pack and leave quickly no one will notice. My heart beats rapidly, then skips a beat ... aha! If I am lucky maybe I can have a heart attack and won't have to sing tonight.

"Schizophrenia, manic depression, moments of total euphoria and then the grovelling in self-pity. I am basically a very introverted person living a very public life.

"When one stands on the stage one is clothed in someone else's skin, a skin moulded by the sweat, love and tears of composer and librettist; but to wear that skin honestly and to make it come to life, one must bare oneself totally. To express any emotion is to bare one's soul naked, stripped of any protective layers. One stands exposed, crying out, 'This is my soul in all its fragility that expresses to you the tragedy, love, sorrow and humor that is packed into our lives. And this is my voice that tried to express what the composer, librettist and my soul have to say.' The voice and the soul. Both intangibles. Yet my voice is the extension of my soul, which is sometimes beautiful and sometimes tired but always, always honest. Treat me gently for my soul is fragile. How vulnerable one is at such a moment; wide open; strengths and weaknesses totally exposed. I ask, why do I do it?

"As I ask myself this question I realize that the answer is that I have no choice. This gift has been entrusted to me; my duty is to give of it to the best of my ability. I am only the instrument of emotion and expression, giving to my fellow man. But I am not prone to analysis. I am a creature of instinct, therefore it is hard for me to verbalize about either my art or why I do it. It seems, however, to have something to do with my search for the absolute."

That self-interview appeared after Teresa had accomplished what may be considered her greatest achievement. She went from Alvin Cooperman's production of *Amahl and the Night Visitors* on NBC-TV to the Paris Opera to sing the title role in Alban Berg's *Lulu*. The event was awaited with even more than the usual anticipation because the complete opera had never before been performed. Berg died before completing the scoring for the third act, which had been reconstructed by the Austrian composer and musicologist Friedrich Cerha.

As the Mother in the film of Amahl and the Night Visitors, *1978.*

Some time before the premiere, *The New York Times* interviewed the star: "Miss Stratas insists that she is not much at analyzing the women she portrays. 'When I analyze a role I always seem to come out with the same answers that my instincts gave me in the first place. But sure, Lulu fascinates me. We see her through the eyes of all those men. Whenever they see another side of her they are always surprised. She has all these facets, and every time a man comes into contact with another side of her, he is destroyed by the discovery.' Doesn't it seem obvious that the outlooks of Lulu and of Teresa are parallel in many ways? 'Well, I find that a man often sees what he wants to see in a woman and then is confused when later he is confronted with all these other sides of her personality. But that's their problem, not mine. I spent a good part of my life asking myself why I couldn't be the things society wanted me to be. Why don't I want to get married, have babies, and so on? But nothing in my life has particularly followed form.'"

Nor was anything usual about that opening night in Paris, February 25, 1979. Some three hundred international music critics were there, along with celebrities from all over the world. The lights dimmed on the bright colors of the Chagall ceiling and then, as Teresa told *Maclean's* magazine.: "I had a fever and was drugged up with cortisone. I didn't want to sing—couldn't sing—but they insisted I did anyway. The cortisone did something to my perspective. Normally I'm myopic, but as I stepped out onto the stage I saw gathered in front of me, so clearly, the entire musical world and the rest of the famous world as well. And then I said to myself, 'So you finally did it. And this is it.' And then I thought, 'So what is it? I suddenly realized that it didn't mean a thing—not—a—thing. So I did what I was supposed to do: I stood there and I sang."

Although the production came in for some inevitable criticism from Berg specialists, the reviews for Teresa were stunning everywhere. Many still call it the musical event of the past several decades. Later, when she performed the role at the Metropolitan Opera in New York, the *Times* of London would send its music critic, Peter Conrad, to compare the production with another *Lulu* then being performed at Covent Garden. Here are some excerpts from his articulate study:

> Directors remain uncertain whether to assign *Lulu* to the 1890s, where Wedekind's plays belong, or to the 1930s, when Berg composed the music. The decision is more than a decorative one. A fin-de-siècle *Lulu* characterizes the heroine as a fatal vamp, a colleague of Beardsley's arachnoid Salome; transferring the action to the 1930s,

as Patrice Chéreau did in Paris in 1979, exonerates her—Chéreau even called her crypto-Jewish, the victim of a slick, greedy bourgeoisie against whose hypocritical pieties she offended. John Dexter's production at the Met situates itself in the ornate perversity of the 1890s. . . .

Handsome though the sets are, they're contradicted by the extraordinary Lulu of Teresa Stratas, for whom the heroine is emphatically not a venereal demon of the 1890s. Her performance attests to Lulu's innocence, even to her moral purity. She sees Lulu not as a genital automaton but as a person who is uniquely and devastatingly honest, and whose beauty terrorizes a society which preserves itself by euphemism and evasion. Lulu doesn't edit or censor her thought. She confides the truth of her feelings—casually advising Alwa that she poisoned his mother or enquiring whether the divan where he's making love to her is the one on which his father bled to death—and her candor can kill.

In a performance of astonishing psychological subtlety, Stratas makes it clear that, though Lulu is a hostage of false morality (she is distressed by the painter's reproving catechism and when he interrogates her about her beliefs can only whimper *'Ich weiss nicht'*) she possesses a moral code of her own to which she is austerely true. Thus she welcomes Jack the Ripper as her savage, surgical redeemer. They are natural allies; with his knife he is cleansing and cauterizing a fouled world, just as she chastens the men who try to own her by contradicting the love which they invent to rationalize their need of her. Jack comes to her as a judge and a murdering conscience, and is accepted as such by the Lulu of Stratas, who kneels before him pleading with him to stay, tenderly petting and bribing him until he condescends to kill her. Lulu envies the dead, as her wondering elegies over the corpses of her three husbands proclaim; and she has an intimacy with death which also joins her to Jack, whose profession is the retributive enforcement of mortality. Stratas's disturbing, touching stage presence perfectly conveys this unearthliness, Wedekind called Lulu an Erdgeist, but it's the spirituality, not the coarse admixture of earth, which Stratas—fragile, thin, with a child's bemused eyes in a ghost's ancient face—represents. Returning from prison, her hair shorn, wasted, her face grey, she speaks with the detachment and the power of divination of those who have been closely acquainted with death by illness.

In her voice, too, there's an eerie ambiguity. Singing, its extensions into the upper register are bright and hysterically shrill, scaling pinnacles of irresponsibility, as in her manic coloratura after the painter's suicide. But when she speaks as in Lulu's plangent appeal to Schön in the second scene, she sounds smoky, grave, almost baritonal, as if two identities, even two sexes, were housed in that slight, tormented body. The Met's Schön and Ripper was Franz Mazura, whose intensity as a singing actor matches that of Stratas. Both Stratas and Mazura dwell on the precipice of what Artaud called danger, the tense and risky arena of self-exposure, and even self-abuse which is reserved to great and daring performers: between them, they ignited the Met's *Lulu.*

No one could be indifferent. Although Teresa's great supporter Rudolf Bing had reservations about the work, he had none about Teresa. In *A Knight at the Opera* he commented: "She gave the performance of her life. Not only was she Lulu, as was to be expected from this extremely talented singing-actress, but she rose to the immense demands vocally, reaching without strain to the top register. It was an amazing performance."

But it is Teresa herself who can best analyze Lulu and what the role has meant to her. Sitting on her couch dappled with many-colored pillows, she unravelled the score. It spread out like an endless accordion. I had asked if perhaps her fascination with death did not indicate a dark spirit. Teresa was unruffled by the question:

"There's a wonderful line in one of the operas I recently have performed. It comes from *Lulu* by Alban Berg and the text is Wedek-ind. He has a fabulous line in there—it's a beautiful musical line too, as a matter of fact. Who it is is not important now, but someone dies, and Lulu says: '*Er hat es überstanden,*' which means he's survived, he's survived it—oh, he's made it. In other words, we still have the struggle ahead of us, but he's made it, he's at peace."

I pushed further: "Does the character of Lulu relate to you personally? In some strong way?"

"Well, I love her very much. I'm very protective of her. I won't let her be that one-sided character. She is more than a one- or two-faceted character. She's been portrayed for so many years as just a vamp. What is a vamp, anyhow? That's boring. She isn't just one color or two colors. She's not a sexual object. She's not just one thing. I think she's all the facets that a person can have in their personality, and I say 'person,' not 'female.' We tend in our society to peg people as being one thing: 'Oh, he's neurotic,' or 'Oh, he's weak,' or 'He's a vicious person.' It's terrible to generalize like that, because people have many characteristics. All of us have. And all of us have the possibility of the spectrum of colors—whether we develop them is something else. She is that total spectrum of the personality, and the music, the complexity of the music of Berg, confirms that. As a matter of fact, when I first received the score of the *Lulu* I couldn't believe it. It hadn't been printed yet." She held up the almost unreadable score. "This is a typical page of the manuscript I was sent from which I should learn the *Lulu*. Isn't that wonderful? I got terrified when I saw the score, and went from pianist to pianist hoping someone was going to help me learn this difficult music. And I couldn't get anyone to teach it to me. I also tried to decipher what the notes were that were on this manuscript. Later they printed a score of it. And this is what my scores now look like. See all these pages—pages and pages of music. This is what one of my scores looks like after I'm finished working with it."

I asked: "Is all of it still in your head?"

She embraced the music: "I've raped it, and loved it and killed it and it's killed me and we've had our battles and whatever else. Yeah … I suppose it is. I don't know. I guess we have a lot of little doors up there and we close some of them occasionally and we open them and hope the right information will come out. At the called time."

The lady was not exaggerating. The passion of Lulu, the passion needed to play Lulu, has caused Teresa as much pain as it has pleasure. This is how she described the Paris production to *The New Yorker*'s Winthrop Sargeant: "We rehearsed ten hours a day, and I had such a feeling of alienation and depression and fright! There was no furniture on the stage. There were some big staircases and little else—just these, a sort of neoclassic, Albert Speer idea. I complained to the director, Patrice Chéreau, and he said, 'That's exactly what I wanted.' If you don't have a set—nothing but those bleak, stark staircases—you're constantly giving so much emotionally. I was dead after every performance. And the other thing he insisted on was that he didn't want me to quote act unquote. I'm a very good actress. He didn't want me to *do*. He wanted me to *be*. So he insisted that I, Teresa Stratas, *be*. We don't go on the stage for that sort of thing. Why are we finally driven to the stage? To get out of ourselves. I put on a costume and I put on someone else's skin, and I go on the stage and escape from myself for those three or four hours. And here was someone who made me stand naked on the stage—literally naked at a few points. But I mean spiritually naked, baring my soul and saying, 'This is me, Teresa Stratas,' and that is very difficult."

Sadly, there is no filmed record of Teresa's New York *Lulu*, because on the very night of the telecast she called in sick. Despite a potential audience of millions, against all possible betting odds, she did not show up.

Following, a sequence of photographs from productions of Lulu *at the Amsterdam Opera, the Paris Opera, and the Metropolitan Opera.*

With Julian Patrick.

With Andrew Foldi.

With Elaine Bonazzi.

With Franz Mazura.

One of the remarkable things about Teresa is that she has been able to do modern opera and the standard *bel canto* repertoire with equal success. For instance, after having sung the Lulus in Paris, she went to Salzburg and sang Mozart—Susanna in *The Marriage of Figaro*. Usually one does not return after a role like Lulu—where the voice is scaling all extremes—to singing the kind of music that needs a sweet sound. I asked Teresa how she could do this.

"I think the reason I've been able to do this is a very basic one. It has a lot to do with my background in that singing isn't just singing to me, but becoming the person. Then it seems like the most normal thing in the world, if I'm Susanna, and I'm about to be married and I'm happy, and I have beautiful lines to sing, to sing them as beautifully as possible. So to bridge and go back isn't all that difficult because I'm never confronted with 'Oh how can I?'—I've become the person so there is no problem."

Hardly was the ink dry on the superlatives for *Lulu* than she was off again with a new vision. In November 1979 she made her debut as Jenny in the Met's new production of *The Rise and Fall of the City of Mahagonny* . The opera had raised a storm in Leipzig when it was first performed in 1930. One man stood on his chair booing and applauding at the same time—it has that kind of divisive power. *Mahagonny* is about lust and greed, about money and the curse it brings. Brecht wrote the libretto as a commentary on the Germany that had come into being after World War I, a place doomed by its own depravity. In Weill's brash and brutal score audiences could feel Nazism rising as the world watched.

The project was a daring one for director John Dexter. Some claimed *Mahagonny* was dated, relevant to only one country at one specific time. Dexter disagreed. Of course, what was going to make it most relevant for operatic audiences was having Teresa in the leading role. But there was one problem. The songs she would sing had been made famous by Weill's widow Lotte Lenya, a huge challenge for Teresa.

Recalling her first impression of *Mahagonny* and Weill's music, Teresa was later to say: "There is something about Kurt Weill that came at the right time for me. I hate categories, and categorization, I really do. And I hate categories in music as well as the labeling of people into convenient stereotypes. I think Kurt Weill said there is only good music and bad music, and all other kinds of categories—popular, classical, etc.—just don't exist; and Weill is all of them. Where does he fit? He's like quick-silver. He's present in all the areas and he's fused them somehow. One of Weill's collaborators, the black

As Susanna in a Covent Garden Nozze di Figaro, *1978. Herbert von Karajan has said, "If you want to sing Mozart properly, listen to Stratas."*

poet Langston Hughes, said he was 'a truly universal artist, who could with equal justice be claimed by Germany as German, France as a Frenchman, by America as an American and by me, as a Negro.' And I responded to him musically because I'd been rejecting a basic part of myself, in my voice and personality, by only being in the world of opera. As a matter of fact, I was actually distressed when I went to the score of *Mahagonny*, because I thought I'd finally have a chance to use my night club voice, which I hadn't used in years, but found out that I had to sing it up there. 'My God', I said, 'do I have to pip it up there?!'"

I asked Teresa what attracted her to Weill. As with Mozart, her favorite composer, one of the qualities she admired was his magnificent humor: "Humor, but humor about—yes, life can be bad, but

In the Met's Maha-gonny, with Arturo Sergi, Philip Eisenberg and Louise Wohlafka, 1979. "As Jenny Miss Stratas is the ultimate in the femme fatale world because she is fatal without needing any embellishments. They're all in her"— The New York Post.

yes, isn't life really quite wonderful, and we should try to keep it going in that direction. I think they both say that very well through their music. I'm not talking about texts now.

"Very often he repeats a melodic line many, many times, and usually if you have a melodic line, even without the text, you're locked into one expression because the line dictates that this is probably the expression—it's happy, it's sad, it's bitter, it's one of those things. Maybe, possibly, two interpretations. And then you usually get the words and that will decide—if there are two possibilities with the music, the words are going to decide which is the expression that's going to go. And the thing about Kurt Weill is . . . I'll give you an example. It's Jenny the prostitute, and she's been asked to bail out her lover by giving him some money, to pay some debts, and she's saying, 'Oh no, I'll give you everything, but I know when I have to save myself.' It's a fight for survival. And she has the following line that comes in the chorus of one of her songs: 'As you make your bed you must lie there and no one will care what you do, and if someone should kick then it's me sir, and if someone gets kicked it will be you.' Now this line can be interpreted in many ways."

Like a teacher with a class Teresa proceeded to explain by singing the line in various versions. The first expression was bitter. Then—"Or you could say, I'm sorry buddy, it was nice knowing you, but

After the premiere of Mahagonny, *with Tony Harrison and the Met's James Levine and Fabrizio Melano.*

you know this is the way life is: 'As you make you bed you must lie there and no one will care what you do.' Or you could think, Isn't it sad, that's how life is: 'As you make your bed you must lie there and'—sorry—'no one will care what you do.' So I found that this recurring theme I could interpret all those ways that a person in life would say it. And not many composers allow you that. As a matter of fact, he's the only one I can think of who does."

I marveled and said: "It's remarkable. Just before we leave this subject, the color of your hair has to do with Lotte Lenya. Does the role—the color of Jenny's hair?"

Teresa leaned back in reflection. Her hair was a defiant orange-red. "Well, I had my hair this color for *Mahagonny.* I had it this color also for *Lulu,* but the last thing was its dark color. Then recently I went to see Lenya and have been spending a good deal of time with her. And my hair is red again.

"The first time I saw Lotte Lenya, we were in rehearsal on the Met stage and I was singing in the role of Jenny. John Dexter was the director. The theater was dark, there was no one in the audience except one person who was sitting in the middle of the audience and John came to me and said, 'Look out in the audience and look very, very carefully right down the middle and you'll see a shock of red hair. That's Lotte Lenya.' I thought I would die. I thought I would go through the stage, that the original—I mean *the* Jenny of the *Mahagonny*, and Kurt Weill's wife, and Lenya, and all of the legend of Lenya—was actually sitting out there, and I was supposed to be doing Jenny. It was very difficult for me. At some point I was introduced to her and she came to the rehearsals every day. And I would go to her and ask her what I'm doing wrong or what she would like, etcetera. She would always say, 'Nothing dear, just keep doing what you're doing.' And I would think, Oh my God, I'm so hopeless, she won't even make any comment, she won't give me any of the knowledge that she carries with her. She just kept saying, 'It's fine dear,' took my hand, 'It's fine, just keep doing what you're doing.' Day in and day out I was sure I must have been absolutely dreadful because she wasn't saying 'It's fabulous' or anything, she was just saying 'No, no, I have nothing to say.' I thought, She has nothing to say because I'm so far away from the right thing. Anyhow, the beginning was very, very—not rocky, but strange. And then we opened and during the run of the *Mahagonny* she had her assistant call me and say, 'Madame Lenya would like to give you some music that has never been performed. She's always kept it locked up in the vaults. She would like you to have it. She'd like to give you some of this music to perform. Would you come and perform a concert in memory of Kurt Weill, at the Whitney Museum?' And I went and sang these songs and I guess Madame Lenya was very pleased, because she then went to the vaults and took everything out, gave me all the unpublished music of Kurt Weill."

Teresa told Louis Morra of *Ovation* magazine: "The Weill album consists entirely of first takes, or at most seconds. I wouldn't allow overdubbing or rerecordings. The studio people, who are not used to doing it that way, protested. My reply was, 'No, this is how I want it, and how it will sound best.' I still can't listen to it. I put it on for a few minutes, tighten up inside, and take it off."

The reviews for the record were superb. *Stereo Review* critic James Goodfriend immediately picked it as "Best of the Month":

> Some records are classics the minute they come out: Dennis Brain playing the Mozart horn concertos, Schwarzkopf and Ackermann doing Strauss' *Four Last Songs*, Richter playing Mussorgsky's *Pictures at an Exhibition*, Yepes and Argenta doing Rodrigo's *Concierto de Aranjuez*. Be the repertoire standard or obscure, the artist well or

A Weill recording session, 1980 (left and above). Of this album High Fidelity *observed that Teresa's only competitor "is her own ghost—past, present and future."*

little known, the elements have come together to produce something new and unique, inherently valuable, immediately communicative, and wearing an aura that assures us it could not have been done better. Such records form a very small, elite group, but they are the justification for the whole record business.

How gratifying it is, then, to apprehend another! A new Nonesuch release, *The Unknown Kurt Weill,* sung by Teresa Stratas, accompanied by Richard Woitach, produced by Eric Salzman, with complete texts and translation, and with extensive notes by Kim Kowalke, is in every way worthy of the most elevated musical company. Frankly, I don't see how it could have been done better. . . .

But all the interest and quality of these songs would be pure, dead ancient history without the spectacular performances of them by soprano Teresa Stratas. If Weill's aesthetic placed dramatic acting far above beautiful singing, here we nonetheless get both. Stratas has an inflection for everything, a vocal coloration for everything. She goes from the tough to the tender in "Nannas Lied" and from the tender to the tough in "Der Abschiedsbrief." Her cries of "Shell! Shell!

Shell!'' in "The Mussel of Margate" move from gentle hucksterism to positive paranoia. She can be cute, hard, sensual, demented, ironic, abstracted, funny, vulgar, aloof, touching, crushing—and through it all *sing* marvelously. Hearing what she can do with a microphone and a piano, one wonders why she drains herself night after night in an opera house. Richard Woitach, who plays the piano here, deserves no little share of the credit; he is as sensitive to mood and meaning as Stratas is. The recording (digital) could not be bettered. The production could not be bettered. The presentation could not be bettered. A classic.

Yet the more successful Teresa became, the more her interviews seemed to point towards approaching retirement. In 1978 she had talked about it with William Littler, the long-time music critic of the *Toronto Star*: "A director once said to me, Teresa, you will never be happy. You are searching for the absolute and it doesn't exist. Well, I don't believe that. I believe it does exist and if we find it, it will be by looking within.

"My life is very public, and I have chosen to spend my few private moments alone. People don't understand this. They think that to be alone is to be lonely. I am also an instinctive artist. This is why I have no desire to teach. People keep asking me how I approach a character. I can't verbalize it and I don't want to. What are art and music? A communication of feeling."

Perhaps no one should have been surprised when Teresa finally decided to pack up and head out on her own for India. Not the India of the tourists—the India of poverty, the India of Mother Teresa. She was trying to find herself. One of the few times she has spoken about the trip in detail was in her interview with Louis Morra: "The world is so immense, with countless lives being lived in endlessly different places, while my personal reality is so small. I found myself rehearsing, performing, coming home, generally living a very safe, sheltered life, and feeling totally isolated and separate from everything beyond that routine. I knew a great deal more was outside, but how was I to get to it? I love to read, but even my books were not helping me escape from feeling trapped.

"Going to India was a release from what looks like a glamorous world of opera engagements. The fact is, it's a proverbial gilded cage, at least for someone whose needs exceed it. It restrained how I felt about myself, my life and my place in the world."

In an interview with Tony Harrison, used on the jacket of her second recording of Weill's songs, Teresa said: "I'll tell you some of the things that I thought were important about India. Some are simple and I'm not quite sure what they're about. The very first day I was there, I walked for about fifteen hours till I was exhausted. I was crazy, manic. Then I wanted to sit down. And as I was stepping around people whose lives took place on the street, eating, pissing, shitting, sleeping, I realized that I could also just sit down there, right on that spot, anywhere. And when I sat down—and this is the truth, I can't really describe it—I had the most incredible feeling, being able to simply sit down. Am I crazy? Say I'm walking on the street, here on Broadway, or on Fifth Avenue, or Park Avenue, and I feel just like sitting down for a few seconds. But I never do. I'd have to look for a bench or a coffee shop. But in India I could sit down anywhere in the street and no one stared at me. It seems a simple thing, but it was immensely important; I thought it might have had something to do with my father having been a shepherd in Crete, sitting down anywhere he liked on his mountain. That happened on the very first day in India. I found a part of myself I'd put aside—no, not put aside, a part of myself felt I had to hide. We are always afraid of doing anything conspicuous or out of step."

In my own conversation with Teresa I asked her to take me through that experience in her own way. I could see in her eyes that she was on that journey again:

"I'm alone, I don't need terribly much to live on. I don't have children or family, and I've been donating a lot of my money to different causes like UNICEF and Mother Teresa. However, as much as we might know about starvation and about disease and about poverty and as many images as we might see on television or in film or in the newspapers, it's something else when you get it first-hand. And when you're actually there you see it.

"This summer I put a backpack on my back and put my sneakers on and took only two dresses with me—one cotton dress I had on, the other was in my backpack—and a few books and things, and I flew to India. I backpacked all the way through India—north, south, east, west, central. I went up into Nepal, into the Himalayas and learned a great, great deal. One of the things I did that was a wonderful experience, for want of another word—wonderful is truly inadequate—I went to the Mission of Charity in Calcutta. And if there's a hell on earth it has to be Calcutta. I mean, the city itself, and the poverty and filth and starvation and pestilence and everything else on the streets. You see your fellow man there, and you have so much and they have absolutely nothing, less than nothing. Dying on the streets. It's truly devastating, and once a person has made such a journey, I think they're never the same. I went to the Mission of

During her travels in India, 1981.

Charity. I wanted to make a donation and I wanted to work in the home for the dying. I had the most incredible experience of my life. The door was answered by one of the younger sisters, and I told her. She said, 'Wait one minute', then one of the older sisters came and she escorted me up some stairs. And there at the top of the stairs stood Mother Teresa. I was so overwhelmed, I hadn't expected to meet her, hadn't asked to meet her, and as you can well imagine I couldn't speak. I was just absolutely ... and she realized it. She realized also that I had a need that brought me there. She held my hand

and she talked to me. I could only sort of nod my head, 'yes' or 'no,' barely talk. I think she managed to get my name out of me and a few other things. But I could barely speak. She said, 'I hear you want to go to the home for the dying and work,' and I said 'Yes.' She said, 'I don't want you to do that, immediately. I'm going to send a sister with you and I'd like you to first go to the orphanage and spend some time there working and playing with the children and then you go to the home for sick children and then after that you can go to the home for the dying.' And I thought that would be interesting too. At that point, I didn't know why she told me to do it that way. At the end of that experience, I certainly knew why. I think if I had gone immediately into the home for the dying, I'm not sure if I would have survived it."

I asked if she had really been totally on her own. She said yes:

"On my own, which is highly unusual—to be a white woman traveling alone. To be a woman, period, traveling alone. But I had incredible experiences. People who were living on the street wanted to share everything with me, total strangers, everybody came up to me and the ones that spoke English tried to ask me questions and offered me their food, all the different foods to try."

I was troubled by the image:

"But people listening to you are going to ask, this lady who lives in New York, who sings at the Metropolitan, what's she doing in the slums of Calcutta?"

"I think it was one of the wisest things I've every done. I think it makes great sense, I think it confirms for me that though I may sing at the Metropolitan Opera, there's no denying that I am my father's daughter and he was a shepherd, a barefoot shepherd in Crete and ... that we are all human beings and we all, I don't know—it sounds corny—we are all one. That is so confirmed in my mind, it is so ... "

Her eyes fixed in space, she continued,

"It was very evident to me that if I came home and got on the great operatic stages of the world and continued to donate as much of my fee as I could, that would be helping. If my fee—one performance fee—goes to Mother Teresa, that money goes a long, long way. Now that it's no longer in the abstract and I know what happens to the money and why I'm up there singing, I feel finally there's a social purpose for my singing." Some years later she said: "Who am I to congratulate myself on my 'artistry' or my musical gift, or the instant celebrity that seems to go with it when that Biafran, or Indian or Ethiopian woman has no milk in her tit to feed her child? But look around us. There are so many people eating out of garbage cans, right here on Broadway, right here in America. How can I close my eyes to this and live only in 'artistic loftiness?'"

Back from India two weeks before rehearsals began at the Metropolitan for *La Bohème*, Teresa telephoned Lotte Lenya, only to learn that she was on her deathbed. "When I came back from India," she told Louis Morra, "it was very important to play Mimi. I felt I was walking forward to her, from India and from roles like Lulu and Salome. It's important to say something positive, even to just one person. Mimi is so frail and good. Mimi was my reaffirmation. It is very dark out there. What she says therefore means a great deal. I tend to look at things angularly. I portray the evil sorts of roles as very real parts of us, but as something to stay away from. Yet the darkness can't simply be shut out, turned away from. You must voice a positive statement with knowledge of the darkness. Then what you say isn't just naive, but becomes a real affirmation against the darkness."

She told me: "We all like to think we're all controlling our fate. Somewhere I feel right now that someone else has got the strings and fate is leading me along a road, a most interesting road. I don't know where it is leading. Yes, I'm not singing to make a career anymore. I've sorted things out and will sing fewer performances, but I truly know the reason I'm singing now."

If I had not been so awed by her spirit, if I had been listening more closely, I might have heard that even then, that night, she was predicting that there would be much less Stratas on view, forecasting a future that would mean much less time at the Met. But I asked another question: "You said once, 'Every time I sing Mimi I feel part of me has died.' Can you explain why you said that? Is it because it was the first? You did it in Canada before you joined the Met."

She answered, deep in thought: "No, I don't know if I feel that particularly about Mimi, or only about each death. I feel there's a little bit, something that I leave there on the stage. A little bit of something from within. I don't know."

I looked about the apartment, trying to settle down from the voyage through her mind. "I notice you've got a few clown figures around the room. Do you link yourself to the clowns?"

She pointed to one harsh orange figure over my head. "Well, I couldn't resist him. I—actually Tony, Tony Harrison—bought me that one. We thought he suited us. He's ugly. We figured no one else would want him, but that he certainly would suit the both of us."

Noticing some pretty clowns caught in the indoor plants, I asked:

Following at right, a sequence of photographs from La Bohème *at the Met with José Carreras, 1981. "Teresa Stratas is a singing actress of presently unrivaled truth"*—The Village Voice.

"How about the marionette figures in the trees?"

"This was given to me. It was made by the stagehands in *Lulu* at the Netherlands Opera and it's supposed to be Lulu in her pierrot, her clown's outfit. And this is from a fan in Germany."

I had noticed another, a strange figure, in the music room. "And there's one in the other room?"

"The one in the cage is there, someone bought me that ... There's a lot of very personal reasons, one of the reasons being that he felt I was a prisoner in my work and of my music and that I would never be able to escape it. As a matter of fact, when he presented it to me he had the door slightly opened and the point was that the clown wouldn't go out. So I keep him in the music room to remind myself that I shouldn't be a prisoner of my work, and that there are a lot more things to life."

The crew reassembled next morning at Teresa's apartment. She was overflowing with energy. First she rehearsed for us some new Weill pieces, which eventually became a second record. When she missed a note she pounded the piano top with a mild expletive. But she found the note.

Then at noon Franco Zeffirelli entered. The master director had come to stage a mini-rehearsal for our cameras. We had tried to arrange for this at the Met itself, but the unions' requests made it impossible. It was a blow, but Franco was anxious to please his star, so he came to us.

With Teresa lying on the couch they rehearsed Mimi's death scene. Folding her hands up and down with a ballet-like gesture, Franco said: "Playing on these hands you get warmth and light from Rodolfo. I might be a hand fetishist. But I think hands are so fundamental for expressing emotions. You can read a person's mind through watching hands. So cling on these hands which are an anchor of safety and comfort and warmth and strength and life."

They rehearsed for an hour or so. Teresa would run through the lyrics, each time giving all, the veins in her forehead pulsing. Then there was a pause. They stood in the mirrored hallway exchanging compliments and confidences .

They were very gentle with each other that day. They needed each other, respected each other, admired each other. There was no indication of future trouble. For the moment, this was a professional romance, star and director becoming one. I felt a little like an intruder.

At *Bohème*'s opening night at the Met, just sitting in the audience left me with a sense of great occasion. I tried to imagine what it would feel like to be on stage, with a few thousand people awaiting every

With the film crew of
StrataSphere.

breath, measuring this performance against every other one, against every other Mimi.

The occasion also had its amusing side for me. My old tuxedo was on its last legs, and just before leaving my hotel I had felt the seat give way. Time had taken its toll. I tried a desperate repair job, but was fully aware that any extreme movement might mean my own shocking entrance at the Met.

The production was a resounding success, intimate where called for, with tears flowing all around, and an absolute circus when Franco wanted spectacle. The audience could not be contained. They were constantly jumping to their feet with bravos for everyone. I would have been jumping myself, except for my delicate condition. But not for a moment did I take my eyes off Teresa. The tiny figure was enormous on stage.

Later I went backstage with hundreds of other people and waited my turn to enter the sanctuary of the dressing room. I think the fans around me would have waited all night for a moment of Teresa's presence. I paid my respects and backed shyly out of the room. I was as star-struck as everyone else.

There was to be one last major filming session. I had wanted desperately to catch the mood of excitement and anxiety backstage during a production. Although at first I had suggested opening night, Teresa decided, wisely, that this might be too much to cope with. So we agreed that the closing performance would be our night at the opera. But it was simple-minded on our part to assume this would be easy. Clem D'Allessio, the resident television production producer at the Met, smiled when I said I would like to film a small piece of the opera. The word came down that we would have to pay a couple of hundred singers and just as many stagehands and musicians if we approached the stage. (The Met is its own empire, with generals and captains at every corner.)

A small compromise was reached. We would be allowed into the dressing room, but only there. Nowhere else. For the privilege of plugging in one small electrical lamp we would be required to have two overtime stagehands observing. The night was set for January 27, 1982. My faithful CBC crew arrived on location at 6:00 P.M., two hours before the curtain was scheduled to rise. I had alerted Ken Gregg, cameraman extraordinary, to be ready for any eventuality. I didn't know exactly what that might be, but my last session with Teresa had taught me to be prepared, and my own street sense, mixed with years of waiting for the "magic moment" of film, demanded that we be ready for anything.

Sometime after 7:00, Teresa darted, a tense bundle of energy, into the dressing room where our camera and lights stood ready. She cleared her throat, and that passed for a greeting. The two stand-by stagehands were sitting by outside—their job for the night. A couple of Met executives also waited in the outer sanctum. I tried talking, but Teresa merely grunted.

It was obvious that talk would not flow. No small talk. No large talk. Apparently this was a kind of ritual prior to performance. So we filmed the many mirrors as Teresa prepared. We saw the transformation from street urchin to opera star as Teresa applied her own make-up. Line by line, color by color. I kept thinking of Cinderella preparing for Prince Charming—but this meeting would be viewed by thousands. I was aware of the whirr of the camera and the sound speaker calling off the minutes. It was like a rocket launch. We filmed one roll ... possibly two. The camera was running out of film.

Then without warning, about ten minutes before curtain time, the fully dressed Mimi opened the door of her dressing room and walked across the hall guarded by the stagehands and Met officials. She approached an elevator that, as I was soon to learn, went to the very bowels of the Met, and called out: "Well, Harry, are you coming?"

I was stunned. The seated stagehands jumped up. The nervous officials were too perplexed to speak. We all crowded like the Marx Brothers into the freight elevator, heading down. In motion, Ken switched film magazines and added the "super-fast" lenses we had brought from Toronto—just in case.

We were clearly in a no-man's-land in terms of Met propriety. But the old stagehands said not a word of protest and the Met officials, I guess, did not dare. We would get to see the distant rehearsal areas as Teresa strolled about testing her vocal cords in the damper atmosphere of the sub-basement. She reached into her costume apron pocket, produced a small tuning whistle, and then let out a musical shriek that would have woken the sleepers in the highest balcony.

As she paced and the camera followed she exclaimed to no one in particular: "A little man sits in your body and occasionally he goes away, goes off on a trip and he's not there, it already disturbs you that he's there, but when he's not there it's much worse." Then another shriek, almost like a wonderful animal. She blew her nose nostril by nostril, like a peasant girl on a Greek hillside . . . and then she spoke again: "All in proper perspective, Mother Teresa and the starving people in India." She sighed, nodded to herself, screamed a musical scream, and the walk along the long corridor was suddenly over. She was prepared to face the audience, and then she sang.

I was almost relieved to see Teresa make it back to her dressing room. The energy she had expended must have burned off ten pounds. There were screams of adulation. We filmed the bowing and autographing that took place as she held court. The admirers glowed in her light. Later we would film a small party in her apartment, with James Levine, Franco, and a few others.

What no one knew that night, except Teresa—and maybe she did not know it herself—was that (at least as of this writing) this would be her last appearance at the Met. By her own complex choice.

I was left to live with the film. The power of Teresa's personality made no peace with the flat screen of our offices in Toronto. Every time we ran through the rushes, the room was full of her presence. I set about trying to film material to blend with our conversation.

Greek festivals and celebrations on the Danforth, a few landmarks like Maple Leaf Gardens, downtown row-houses cramped together against the Canadian winter. Down to Scarborough Bluffs to catch a coastline that could have been the cliffs of Crete. I also wanted to use excerpts from various opera films that Teresa had performed in. At first I met resistance on the part of some owners. But one phone call from Teresa and the film became available. With Ken Gregg we mixed color filters as we had in the Chagall film. Then, Chagall had suggested that "the colors must whistle." Now, the song must have colors.

As for Teresa, she had agreed to go to Rome and film *La Traviata* with Franco.

I had planned a trip to Greece to retrace the steps Teresa's father had taken in his pilgrimage to Canada. But the timing was difficult because of Teresa's shooting schedule, which seemed to get longer and longer as stories of trouble and temper began to drift out of Rome. Meanwhile, the film was still not complete.

There were a few trans-Atlantic phone calls. I received an honorary degree from the University of Toronto. It was important, more important than any of the hundred other prizes that had come my way. I felt it was a tribute to my immigrant parents and what they had suffered—and to all immigrant parents. Where would we have been without their desire to see us find a better life?

In June I wrote again:

> I hope by the time this letter has arrived events have settled down for you on the film. You sounded surrounded when last we spoke. I am sure that when the smoke dies down and Franco eases off it will be quite beautiful.
>
> Meantime, I thought I would express a few thoughts about the film. I am in a way feeling quite sad it is nearing completion. There is that creative sadness that comes when you feel you've hit all the right notes and then gone beyond. Up there in a kind of Stratas-Sphere in this case. Yesterday we did a temporary sound mix. At the moment we are running some 90 minutes and there is some material in the film that we do not have rights to—such as a brief sequence from the Met production on stage of *La Bohème*. But the film still needs an ending. . . .

By early July I was able to tell Teresa that, because of the enormous enthusiasm of everyone who had seen the rough cut, the film was to run ninety minutes and that a telecast date had been set: January 2, 1983. Now I was more anxious than ever for her to see the film and help me decide on the ending.

Summer gave way to fall. Meanwhile, I had filmed Mother Teresa at a mass rally at Toronto's Varsity Stadium. Through a long focal-length lense, in slow motion, Mother Teresa would appear to be almost walking on air, moving directly towards us but never arriving, being there but not actually on this earth. It suited the mood perfectly. Said the painter Degas: "The real traveler is the man who never arrives."

The shot was not unlike the not-arriving Teresa. I made one last attempt to involve her again in the film:

> Dear Sister Teresa,
> Welcome back from the wilds of Florida to the wilds of New York. Obviously, you know I have been trying to get hold of you. In the event you are reading your mail, this is why.
> You are great. The film is great. But I really have to make a final decision about finishing it. Crews have been booked ... studios have been reserved ...
> We ran the rough cut of the film for some select critics here last week and the comment heard was "She is beautiful, the film is beautiful." I don't wish to impose on your privacy or your desire for seclusion but if you could call at the office number it would help straighten out matters.
> I just want this film to be the best one yet.

StrataSphere would be finished in its unfinished state. We locked up the film. Mixed the tracks with the great Joe Grimaldi, "the maestro," and experimented with the sound so that the background would sometimes dominate, the music driving, penetrating, exclaiming like a great human outcry. I watched the broadcast at home in the company of my wife and a visitor from New York, Al Wasserman. A talented colleague from my early days at CBS, he was now producer of the popular "60 Minutes" program. We shared a Chinese dinner and sat before the set. I was anxious to catch up on the news of friends with whom we had worked in what is now called the "Golden Age" of television. But he shushed me up: "Listen, listen, what she is saying is so interesting." I think Al envied me the opportunity of making a ninety-minute film about a figure like Teresa, now that the U.S. networks are convinced that in a world where anyone can be a star for twenty minutes, no film need be any longer than that.

The first phone call was from the distinguished Canadian contralto Maureen Forrester, high in praise of her fellow star. A note was jammed into our mail box from an unknown neighbor that snowy night, saying simply, "Thank you. Oh, thank you so much"—in our own arch-quiet area of Rosedale, in conservative Toronto, this was the equivalent of fireworks. And at subsequent screenings—at the World Film Festival in Montreal, the Metropolitan Museum in New York, the Smithsonian Institution in Washington, the Mill Valley Film Festival near San Francisco, and, eventually, the Academy Awards presentation, where it received the Certificate of Special Merit—the reactions were similar. Some would come hundreds of miles to see Teresa on film. Some would not be able to contain their sorrow. There could be no more powerful accolade.

The reviews were even better than I had hoped. From *Maclean*'s Bill MacVicar: a "hypnotic portrait of this seemingly imploding star. A glimpse of a personality of command and beauty"; from *The Globe and Mail*'s Jay Scott: "Stratas uses the opportunity to hold the audience's heart in the palm of a tiny, pale hand, and bear it aloft on the rapturous tones of a huge, magically variegated voice"; from columnist Wessley Hicks: "She is a presence. She owns the screen. She owns the stage when she sings. For all her protestations and expressions of doubt, she owns Teresa Stratas."

As for Teresa, she would not view the film. I sent reports. I also kept in touch with the launching of the *Traviata* film. *New York Times* critic Vincent Canby tossed bouquets to Teresa, concluding: "It's an acting performance of breathtaking intensity. It's so good that it eclipses, for the moment anyway, the memory of Greta Garbo in *Camille*, George Cukor's 1937 adaptation of the Dumas play that was also the basis of Piaves' libretto for Verdi."

I attended the opening arranged by the owner of the Plaza Theater, Ralph Donnelly. Fans crammed outside the theater on 58th Street, waiting for the stars. Placido Domingo took his bows. But Teresa was nowhere in sight. Franco entered escorting some vintage film star. I had not seen him since we parted at Teresa's apartment the night of the last *Bohème*. I put my hand out and tried to smile: "Our lady is not here." He withdrew his hand. A quick look of anger crossed his face. He turned away brusquely and said: "Perhaps 'your lady,' but not mine."

In spite of the differences between Teresa and Franco about *Traviata*, this is how Franco's autobiography describes his reaction to the film at its New York opening on April 20, 1983:

Following, a sequence of photographs from Franco Zeffirelli's film of La Traviata, *1983.*

With Placido Domingo.

With Cornell MacNeil.

With Placido Domingo.

In the darkness of the theatre I gradually realized that there was a noise like a distant tide from the audience. People were crying quite openly, and not just the women. In the half-light, I could make out people fumbling for handkerchiefs and tissues as they fought to control their feelings. I looked back at the screen as Violetta struggled to convince Alfredo and herself that she was not dying, that she could get up, and that they would be able to live together again. Then I knew that, despite all the odds, Teresa had created the Violetta we had all been dreaming of. I looked at *her* wide, dark eyes begging for a little more time to live and love, and then I realized that I too was crying, quite helplessly.

The curtain was lowered in triumph.

Act Three

After an intermission of four years, the curtain rises again. Teresa had vanished, just as she had talked about in so many interviews. Rumor had her living in a shed in northern Florida, tending her ailing father, visiting Tony Harrison in a small English village in total anonymity. She was everywhere, living her life, and she did not sing a note in public. The great opera houses awaited her return.

In *Demented: The World of the Opera Diva*, Ethan Mordden wrote of Teresa's disappearance:

> The most consistent canceler of the modern age is Teresa Stratas— unfortunately, for she is one of the distinctive artists, always different, always opulent, and, among other things, the unrivaled Lulu of her time. Considering that this is the essential diva role in *the* post-Romantic masterpiece, and that Stratas was chosen, virtually inevitably, to create the world premiere when Berg's third act finally slipped out of his widow's mad eyrie, this is quite a credential. Stratas' friends would warn her that her self-willed and spontaneous behavior would get her into trouble, for the backstage of opera is calculated and Stratas is alive, self-propelled. Yet she must hold the record not only for quantity but quality of cancellations, as when she canceled Lulu in a "Live From Lincoln Center" telecast. Even Montserrat Caballé, Stratas' most potent contender in the sweepstakes, has not pulled off anything as magnificent. Caballé has instigated near-riots for no-shows at La Scala, but this means disappointing thousands. A Met telecast involves millions. Having scaled this Everest of indispositions, Stratas had nothing left to cancel but her career; and did. How can such an exciting singer live without singing?

With Tony Harrison. "Few voices have such an identifiable plangent, vibrant timbre," wrote The Wall Street Journal, *lamenting her disappearance from the stage.*

To understand, or attempt to understand, Teresa's absence, we might look for a moment at the female opera star. We think of a prima donna as a woman who is temperamental, who wants her own way—a living tantrum. The fact is that opera has always operated on the high wire of emotions. Maria Malibran, Jenny Lind, Adelina Patti, Nellie Melba, Geraldine Farrar—these were Teresa's antecedents. Each one brought the image of the diva to new heights. English musiologist Rupert Christianson outlines that progress in his book *Prima Donna*:

> The prima donna became a grander creature towards the end of the [nineteenth century] . . . . Some of these singers could act quite powerfully when they chose, yet any attempt at presenting ordinarily credible or consistent human behavior on stage was generally eschewed, as the prima donna regularly broke out of character to acknowledge applause and any other sort of tribute. There was little respect for accurate musical texts. Cuts and wanton transpositions were common. The prima donna could sing as much as she chose, and conductors and colleagues had to follow suit. Touring the voracious new American market, and later, recording doubled her money. Her social position consolidated itself, simply because no one could gainsay her. Talent, money, and popularity made up for birth.

While musical standards have probably become more exacting with time, such power still brings with it many conflicts—especially between the desire to satisfy one's public and the need for independence. Ethan Mordden has observed:

> Independence pays different prices in different eras, but always the most self-willed divas, given the talent to back up their claims, are the most famous. They are not always loved. Malibran was, but Schroder-Devrient was rather admired, Garden was misunderstood, Olivero was regarded as pleasant camp, and Scotto is disliked. Does opera want independence?
>
> Impresarios don't. Most stage directors don't. Most critics don't; they want everyone as vapid as they are themselves. The maestro is the only member of the staff who needs a diva to make the wild magic, who is as much a part of the music as she is. . . .
>
> Different times know different rules. One rule, however, has held from then to now: independence is marvelous and dangerous. We have our wise Freni and Horne, imperturbably superb; but we also have Stratas, who dares. Stratas seems as wary of independence as determined upon it—she sees its traps. Perhaps she knows the story of Malibran, who sang herself to death.

So each prima donna is a story and a legend. They have been worshipped and mocked in films from *Citizen Kane* to *Luna* to *Diva*.

But virtually all comparisons lead to the other Greek, Maria Callas. I asked Teresa if they had had any encounter. She said, "She phoned here once. I'm basically a very introverted person. It takes me a long time to pick up the phone to phone someone, but I'd gone to one of her lectures here in New York City, and my curiosity about something she said was greater than my introversion, and I picked up the phone and called her at the hotel. She wasn't in. And I left a message, and she phoned here. I had a broadcast matinee the next day, I had seen the lecture Friday night, Saturday afternoon I was singing at the Met. And I think she phoned in those hours because she knew I wouldn't be home. And she spoke to a friend of mine who was in the apartment, and said, tell Teresa that the most important thing . . . no, she asked is Teresa happy, and the person answered as best as he could, and she said, tell Teresa it's very important to be happy, to take care of herself. And she left a very beautiful message, and then of course, I was too shy to call back when I got home. And I received one letter from her once, very cherished."

The long intermission in Teresa's career seemed as necessary to her as performance had been for all the years before. I had written her that I was going to show *StrataSphere* at the Metropolitan Museum of Art and speak on the subject of passion. She wrote back from Florida: "Passion sounds like a really good topic for your lecture, Harry, maybe Pain and Passion (Passion and Pain?) and daring to feel both, though God knows, I'd give anything right now to cut out at least the pain part. Oh, well life is a pain isn't it? Thank heavens for our sense of humor." The letter was signed with no return address.

Finally, in 1986, she sang again. Surprising everyone, she accepted the starring role in a Broadway musical called *Rags*, the story of a Jewish immigrant family just after the turn of the century. In a sense, she was singing the story of her own family's pilgrimage to the new land—but now she was the mother.

Teresa's career decisions have always been unexpected. Despite many offers in the interim, Teresa's silence was not broken until the winter of 1986, when she was approached by three talented and highly successful men: Charles Strouse, composer of such Broadway hits as *Bye Bye Birdie*, *Applause*, and *Annie* (and a former student of Nadia Boulanger and Aaron Copland); Stephen Schwartz, lyricist of *Pippin* and *Godspell*; and Joseph Stein, author of *Fiddler on the Roof*. When they told her their plan, Teresa said that a musical was the last thing she ever wanted to do. The reason she agreed to consider it was the theme: the immigrant experience.

As Rebecca in Rags, *at the Mark Hellinger Theater, 1986. With Josh Blake (above).*

"They sent me a tape with some of the songs," she told the *New York Times*' Heidi Waleson in an interview shortly before the Broadway opening. "I put it on thinking I was going to turn it off in a second, and I had to sit down and listen." Still she was not convinced: "I was afraid it might trivialize an important subject and, because it was Broadway, try to make it light, pasteurize the pain of the immigrants so that God forbid anyone might really feel anything like what the immigrants actually felt. But they promised they were really going to risk it . . . ."

Teresa set tough terms for her participation, especially creatively. She wanted to contribute what she knew about the character of Rebecca, the mother of us all. She told Waleson: "They let me speak from my own experience. Rebecca is really from my own mother, what I've told the men about a woman like that, and what she did for her children."

It looked like a dream situation. But as someone once said, the way to defeat Hitler would have been to send him on the road with a musical on its way to Broadway. *Rags* was to be directed by Joan

Micklin Silver, who had written and directed the film *Hester Street*; however, she had never faced the challenge of a musical, and this one was coming in for approximately five million dollars. After only three weeks of rehearsals, Silver was gone. The company headed for the traditional Boston try-out run without a director (Strouse and Schwartz took charge) and with a script that was still being revised.

Along with everything else, Teresa had to adjust to the artificial amplification of her voice: "After spending thirty years of my life learning to make my crescendos and decrescendos when I want them, I'm not crazy about some one else controlling my sounds," she said in the *Times* interview.

The reviewers sang her praises, and during the final week in Boston, the show played to capacity crowds. Teresa received standing ovations every night.

Opening night in New York had a Jewish heart about it, but also the shadow of Greek tragedy. It would be up to the critics. Correction: to one critic. A show of the dimensions of *Rags* could never survive without an almost total rave from Frank Rich, the current maker and breaker of theatrical fortunes at *The New York Times*. And although the opening-night audience was delighted, the *Times* critic would not be moved. Yet of Teresa he wrote:

"It was a smart idea to cast this diva as Rebecca, all right—but ... a risky one too. When the star's voice and spiritual fire blast out of her frame, the show must be ready to match her eruption for eruption. . . ."

The review concluded with a tribute to her, but the final message was grim. As she dances, Rich wrote, "one sees the ghost of another Weill champion, Lotte Lenya, whose Broadway turn in *Cabaret* twenty autumns ago was marked by another charming party dance sequence. . . . Miss Stratas, like her predecessor, is an unexpected and highly welcome immigrant to the popular stage. But life on Broadway is not always a cabaret."

Clive Barnes, once the resident dance and drama critic at the *Times*, now has the same position over at the afternoon *Post*. Although he too found the book a major problem, he had warm praise for the cast, especially Teresa:

"She plucks out the truth in this tinsel, the passion in this pastiche, and she acts and sings with a consummate, heroic identification she did not even bring to Berg's opera *Lulu* at the Metropolitan. . . . Broadway is not accustomed to her voice."

Unfortunately, these days the *Post* has little power.

It was decided to close the show on Saturday night. In order to keep it alive, Teresa offered to sing without salary until the show had a chance to catch on with the public. When the rest of the cast found out, they followed suit, even though it would mean no bread and butter on many a table. But what was needed here was a million dollars, in a hurry. The curtain came down forever on Saturday night.

Ironically, in May, 1987, *Rags*—after just four performances—was the only American show nominated for the best-musical Tony award and of the three nominees for best actress in a musical, one was Teresa. And later that month, Teresa received the award for best actress in a musical for her role in *Rags* by the Drama Desk, a prestigious association of New York drama critics, writers, and reporters.

Meanwhile, a second recording of Weill songs appeared to ecstatic reviews in the fall of 1986. The *Times* of November 30 ran a picture with its critique, the haunting face, both lined and lovely, staring out with the eyes of a wise child from under the newsboy cap. The last paragraph could have summed up more than the recording itself:

> The chemistry between Kurt Weill and Teresa Stratas ultimately resides in this shared adaptability, which is far more than just a matter of style. It is rooted in a deep human empathy. With songs that range from marching ditties to lavish Viennese waltzes, orchestrations that run from a ragtag brass band to sumptuous late Romantic operatic, and singing that soars to the heavens and grovels in the dirt (sometimes almost in the same breath), *Stratas Sings Weill* has a multitude of voices. . . . It is a record filled with the richness of life.

In recent years I've held many public screenings of *StrataSphere*, reliving with enthusiastic new audiences the making of the film. After all this time, Teresa still haunts me. Just as she once vanished from the world of opera without an explanation, keeping her reasons to herself, so she has recently begun to perform again as if she had never left. In the summer of 1987 she recorded the role of Julie in Jerome Kern's classic 1927 musical *Showboat*, along with Frederica von Stade and Jerry Hadley. As is the case with anything Teresa does, this recording promised to be more than a conventional crossover album, restoring dialogue and songs that were cut from the original production in its pre-Broadway try-outs. The reviews have been glowing, with the *New York Times* praising "its vital, intense performances, especially Miss Stratas' Julie." Teresa has also been active again in the opera house. In February 1988, she sang Lulu, the role she has been so identified with, at the Théâtre Royal de la Monnaie of the Belgian Opéra National in Brussels, in a controversial, surreal production by

A Chaplinesque moment in the Brussels Lulu *(right). Recording* Showboat, *1987 (left). Alan Rich wrote: "The Stratas Julie, like the Stratas Lulu or the Stratas Kurt Weill, is the incomparable dramatic creation of an artist with an uncanny ability to get under your skin at every turn of phrase ... a phenomenal artist."*

East German director Ruth Berghaus. Teresa received rave reviews across Europe, in major newspapers in Germany, France, Belgium, Holland, Austria and England, and in *Opera News*. Then, as if to repeat her previous feat of going from Berg to Mozart, she went on to star in a European film of *Cosi fan tutte* directed by Jean-Pierre Ponnelle. And just the other day I read in the morning paper that Tony Harrison is writing a play for her, which is scheduled next spring at the National Theatre in London. So Teresa continues to amaze and delight audiences, a great artist who will undoubtedly become a legend. We can only sit back and wait to see—and hear—what she does next.

The final image in StrataSphere—*as Jenny in the Met's* Mahagonny.

Recordings

Many of the following records are available only in Europe or in record stores that deal with imports. Recordings listed in the current Schwann catalog are marked *.

COMPLETE OPERAS

Berg
Lulu (with Franz Mazura and Yvonne Minton; Paris Opera Orchestra, Pierre Boulez, conductor; Deutsche Grammophon).

Leoncavallo
I Pagliacci (with Placido Domingo; La Scala Orchestra and Chorus, Georges Prêtre, conductor; Philips). Film soundtrack.

Mozart
Cosi fan tutte (with Kiri Te Kanawa and Frederica von Stade; Strasbourg Philharmonic Orchestra, Alain Lombard, conductor; Pantheon).

Le Nozze di Figaro (with Sena Jurinac, Teresa Berganza and Sesto Bruscantini; Zubin Mehta, conductor; Legendary Recordings). A pirated recording of a live performance in 1968; the orchestra is not identified.

Smetana
The Bartered Bride (with René Kollo and Walter Berry; Münchner Rundfunkorchester, Jaroslav Krombholc, conductor; Eurodisc). Film soundtrack.

Verdi
La Traviata (with Placido Domingo and Cornell MacNeil; Metropolitan Opera Orchestra; James Levine, conductor; Elektra Records). Film soundtrack.

La Traviata (with Fritz Wunderlich and Hermann Prey; Bavarian State Opera, Antonino Votto, conductor; Historical Recording Enterprises). A pirated recording from 1965.

COMPLETE OPERETTAS

Léhar
The Merry Widow (with Elizabeth Harwood and René Kollo; Berlin Philharmonic, Herbert von Karajan, conductor; Deutsche Grammophon).

Paganini (with Antonio Theba; Das Symphonie Orchester Kurt Graunke, Wolfgang Ebert, conductor; Philips). Film soundtrack.

Der Zarewitsch (with Wieslow Ochman; Das Symphonie Orchester Kurt Graunke, Wolfgang Ebert, conductor; Philips). Film soundtrack.

MUSICALS

Kern
Showboat (with Frederica von Stade and Jerry Hadley; London Sinfonietta, John McGlinn, conductor; Angel-EMI).

EXCERPTS AND HIGHLIGHTS

Granville-Hicks
Nausicaa (with the Athens Symphony Orchestra, Carlos Surinach, conductor; CRI).

Verdi
Otello, in German (with Wolfgang Windgassen and Dietrich Fischer-Dieskau; Bavarian State Orchestra, Otto Gerdes, conductor; Deutsche Grammophon).

RECITALS

Weill
The Unknown Kurt Weill (with Richard Woitach, piano; Nonesuch Records).

Stratas Sings Weill (with the Y Chamber Symphony, Gerard Schwartz, conductor; Nonesuch Records).

Miscellaneous
Hermann Prey: Musik ist meine Welt (EMI). Stratas was a guest artist on Prey's recital album.

Pirated
The Unknown Teresa Stratas (Legendary Recordings).

Parnassus Recordings presents the renowned soprano Teresa Stratas (Parnassus Recordings).

VIDEO
The following titles are readily available in North America. Many of Stratas's other opera films are available on video cassette only in Europe.

Amahl and the Night Visitors (with Giorgio Tozzi and Nico Castel; Philharmonia Orchestra, Jesus Lobez-Cobos, conductor; Arvin Brown, director; Video Arts International).

La Bohème (with José Carreras and Renata Scotto; Metropolitan Opera Orchestra, James Levine, conductor; Franco Zeffirelli, director; Metropolitan Opera Videos).

I Pagliacci (with Placido Domingo; La Scala Orchestra and Chorus, Georges Prêtre, conductor; Franco Zeffirelli, director; Philips Classics).

Salome (with Astrid Varnay and Vienna Philharmonic Orchestra, Karl Böhm, conductor; Götz Friedrich, director; Unitel).

La Traviata (with Placido Domingo and Cornell MacNeil; Metropolitan Opera Orchestra, James Levine, conductor; Franco Zeffirelli, director; MCA Home Video).

Acknowledgments

O, Canada. None of this would have been possible without the sometime maddening and wonderful land that pained us so and yet gave us the chance to become what we are. For that I must be grateful. And grateful, also, to the CBC, for allowing me to make films such as *StrataSphere* — especially to Hugh Gauntlett and Ivan Fecan, who have been such thoughtful supporters these last years. Thanks also to my film crew: the always steady Ken Gregg, Johnny Maxwell, Erik Kristensen, Erik Hoppe, and Geoff Cheesebrough; Paul Nikolich for his magnificent editing; my faithful deputies, in the past Aili Suurallik and now Patricia Bustine; and Shirley Harris for typing with a smile. Sound mix by maestro Joe Grimaldi, dazzling color by all-seeing Jimmy Lo, photos courtesy of Fred Phipps.

Loving Arlene, as always, found the story and encouraged me to go on; our now almost-adult kids, Holly and Adam, tolerated my work. I am also grateful to my book agent, Lucinda Vardey, who really is a giant of Canadian literature, at home on the piano as well as with the contract. Most especially, I must thank Oxford's literate, capable managing editor, Richard Teleky, who inspired the book and me. He made it almost easy.

SIR RUDOLPH BING, excerpts from *A Knight at the Opera* and *5000 Nights at the Opera* used by permission of the author. RUPERT CHRISTIANSEN, excerpts from *Prima Donna* (1986). Used by permission of The Bodley Head. PETER CONRAD, excerpt from *Times* review © Peter Conrad. Used by permission of Watkins/Loomis Agency, Inc. JAMES GOODFRIEND, excerpt from *Stereo Review* (November 1981). Used by permission. WILLIAM LITTLER, excerpts from *Toronto Star* 3 December 1978. Used by permission. ETHAN MORDDEN, passages from *Demented: The World of the Opera Diva* by Ethan Mordden: copyright © 1984 by Ethan Mordden. Reprinted by permission of the author. WINTHROP SARGEANT, excerpts from "Presence". Reprinted by permission; © 1981 by Winthrop Sargeant. Originally in *The New Yorker*. FRANCO ZEFFIRELLI, *Zeffirelli: An Autobiography*. Reprinted by permission of Weidenfeld & Nicolson, New York, A Division of Wheatland Corporation. Copyright © 1986 by Interfilm Finance SA.

Photo Credits

Front and back covers: Copyright © Beth Bergman. Frontispiece: Paul Ronald. Page vii: Copyright © Beth Bergman. 6: © Helaine Messer. 9: CBC. 12: Private collection. 17: CBC. 30: © Oda Sternberg. 32: Life Picture Service. 34: © Dimitri. 35, 36: Private collection. 37: Copyright © Beth Bergman. 38: Louis Melançon, Metropolitan Opera House. 40: © Paul Filipp. 41 (top): Rudolf Betz, München. 41 (bottom): Louis Melançon, Metropolitan Opera House. 42: Winnie Klotz, Metropolitan Opera Association. 43: Copyright © Beth Bergman. 44: © Arthur Grimm. 45 (top): Paul Smith. 45 (bottom): ZDF, 46: Copyright © Beth Bergman. 47: © Harry Weber. 48: Sabine Toepffer, München. 49: Paul Ronald. 50: Copyright © Beth Bergman. 52–54: © Lars Looschen. 56: Canadian Opera Company, O'Keefe Center. 59: Used by permission of Alvin Cooperman. 64–67: © copyright Jaap Pieper. 68: Copyright © Beth Bergman. 69: *L'Express*—Jean Pierre Couderc, Paris, France. 70, 71: Copyright © Beth Bergman. 73: Christina Burton. 74, 75: Copyright © Beth Bergman. 76: Private collection. 78, 79: Keith Holzman/Nonesuch. 82: Private collection. 85 (top) Copyright © Beth Bergman. 85 (bottom): © Henry Grossman. 86–88: Copyright © Beth Bergman. 90: Private collection. 96–98: Paul Ronald, 100: © Henry Grossman. 104: Carol Rosegg/Martha Swope Associates. 105: Robert Schwartz. 108: Clive Barda. 109: © Jaap Pieper. 110: Winnie Klotz, Metropolitan Opera Association.

Every effort has been made to determine and contact copyright owners. In the case of any omissions, the publisher will be pleased to make suitable acknowledgments in subsequent editions.